C. C. A. CHRISTENSEN

Introductions to Mormon Thought

Edited by Matthew Bowman and Joseph M. Spencer

For a list of books in the series, please see our website at www.press.uillinois.edu.

C. C. A. CHRISTENSEN

A Mormon Visionary

JENNIFER CHAMPOUX

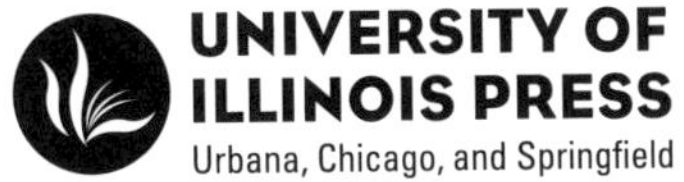
UNIVERSITY OF ILLINOIS PRESS
Urbana, Chicago, and Springfield

Manufactured in the United States of America
1 2 3 4 5 C P 5 4 3 2 1
♾ This book is printed on acid-free paper.

Cataloging data available from the Library of Congress
LCCN 2026932217
ISBN 978-0-252-04956-9 (cloth ; alk.)
ISBN 978-0-252-08921-3 (paper : alk.)
ISBN 978-0-252-04871-5 (ebook)

The manufacturer's authorized representative in the EU for product safety is Mare Nostrum Group B.V., Mauritskade 21D, 1091 GC Amsterdam, The Netherlands. Email: gpsr@mare-nostrum.co.uk

Contents

Foreword to the Introductions to Mormon Thought Series

Our purpose in this series is to provide readers with accessible and short introductions to important figures in the intellectual life of the religious movement that traces its origins to the prophetic career of Joseph Smith, Jr. With an eye to the many branches of that movement (rather than solely to its largest branch, The Church of Jesus Christ of Latter-day Saints), the series gathers studies of what scholars have long called *Mormon* thought. We define "thought" and "intellectual life," however, quite as broadly as we define "Mormonism." We understand these terms to be inclusive, not simply of formal theological or scholarly work, but also of artistic production, devotional writing, institutional influence, political activism, and other nonscholarly pursuits. In short, volumes in the series assess the contributions of men and women who have shaped how those called Mormons in various traditions think about what "Mormonism" is.

We hope that this series marks something of a coming of age of scholarship on this religious tradition. For many years, Mormon studies have focused primarily on historical questions largely of internal interest to the (specifically) Latter-day Saint community. Such historical work has also mainly addressed the nineteenth century. Scholars have accordingly established the key sources for the study of Mormon history and culture, and they have established a broad consensus on many issues surrounding the origins and character of the religious movement. Recent work, however, has pushed academics into the work of comparison, asking larger questions in two key ways. First, recent scholars have approached these topics from a greater variety of disciplines. There has emerged in Mormon studies, in other words, increasing visibility for the disciplines of philosophy, sociology, literary criticism, and media studies, among others. Second, scholars working this field have also begun to consider new topics of study—in particular, gender and sexuality, the status of international Mormonism, and the experience of minority groups within the tradition. We believe the field has thus reached the point where the sort of syntheses these books offer is both possible and needed.

The central argument of Champoux's book links it to these purposes. Christensen's work as an early Mormon artist became popular because of his visceral familiarity with that which he painted. Christensen arrived in Utah ten years after the Mormons arrived in the territory, and he was personally familiar with many of the Saints who had crossed the plains and known Joseph Smith. Indeed, his migration predated the laying of the railroad and, thus, he walked across the Midwestern plains himself. Like many other nineteenth-century Mormons, he was a jack of all trades, whose spiritual life, financial life, and political life were one and the same. He supported himself as a farmer in Utah, but also moonlighted as a newspaper editor, teacher, and politician. He received some art training but also developed his own style, one which blended his formal European training with his fascination with the Western landscape and the narratives of his faith. Champoux thus argues that Christensen is not merely significant as a Latter-day Saint artist, but also as one who stands at the crossroads between Western landscape art, European professional style, and the Mormon experience.

Matthew Bowman
Joseph M. Spencer

Acknowledgments

One of the artworks I remember most from my childhood is a large reproduction of C. C. A. Christensen's *The Handcart Company*. Framed in rustic wood, the piece hung in the front room of the bunkhouse at the family ranch in Emery County, Utah. Perhaps I saw my own Scandinavian pioneer heritage reflected in the painting. My annual visits to the ranch tied me to the history of ancestors who settled similar areas in the region. Although, as a girl from an eastern city, on those trips I was also a visitor in a strange land where the familiar might suddenly slip into the mysterious.

Writing this book has been a similar experience. C. C. A.'s art and writing tell the story of a man with a vision of how the world could be and a willingness to dedicate his life to making it a reality. It is the kind of discipleship I aspire to. And yet, there are parts of his story—such as his practice of polygamy or his representations of Indigenous people—that today feel uncomfortable. I look now at *The Handcart Company* with a fuller understanding of the complexities of history. But I am still moved by the way C. C. A. documented in it, and in so much of his art, ordinary people choosing an extraordinary path.

This book began as conference presentations at the 2019 Mormon Scholars in the Humanities conference and the 2021 and 2022 Mormon History Association conferences. I am grateful to all who offered feedback at these presentations. Among them, my special thanks go to Devan Jensen, who introduced me to the Hancock and Huntington Panoramas and continues to be a delightful scholarly collaborator; Samuel Brown, who generously shared his notes on Book of Mormon wilderness with me; and Richard Oman, who talked with me about his extensive research on C. C. A.

I am indebted to Laura Paulsen Howe and Carrie Snow at the Church History Museum, to Benjamin Whisenant at the Church History Library, and to Ashlee Whitaker Evans and Tiffany Wixom at the Brigham Young University Museum of Art. With their help, I was able to examine original paintings, study archival and curatorial documents, and secure image permissions. Ardis Parshall generously sent me transcribed letters or information uncovered in her voluminous historical research. I'm particularly grateful to Michael Austin for inviting me to present a lecture on C. C. A. at Snow College in 2024, and to his wife, Karen, for helping me hunt down pioneer-era sources and landmarks in Ephraim. Michael's incisive comments and careful edits on the full manuscript improved it tremendously, and he suggested the perfect book title. Katherine Carroll provided valuable developmental editing on early drafts of several chapters. Joey Stuart created a helpful and thorough index for the book.

Series editors Matt Bowman and Joe Spencer offered mentorship and thoughtful ideas to expand my analysis. When I doubt my academic chops, I remember the confidence they expressed in my abilities by bringing me onto this series. That support helped me move forward both in this project and others. I am forever grateful. Alison Syring at the University of Illinois Press made the project a joy with her perfect blend of kindness and professionalism. Thank you to Leigh Ann Cowan, Tad Ringo, Tamira Butler-Likely, Jennie Fisher, the UIP board, the anonymous reviewers for very helpful feedback, and everyone else who helped see this book through to publication.

A publication grant from the Charles Redd Center for Western Studies at Brigham Young University made it possible to include the stunning full-color images in this volume. I'm grateful to the Redd Center for also awarding me a research grant early in the project.

It was an unexpected delight to connect with several descendants of C. C. A. through this project, including Jennett Labrum, Linda Wardle, and Maren Pratt. These lovely women were enthusiastic about my project and provided important information.

My deepest thanks, of course, go to my family. My children—Justin, Brooke, and Jack—constantly amaze me. There is nothing I love more than examining the world with them. Their support of my work on this book means so much to me. It was my parents, Woody and Page Johnson, who fostered my love of art. I'm grateful for their constant encouragement.

My sisters, Erin and Katie, inspire me with the good work they do. My grandparents, Glendon and Bobette, who hung that pioneer painting at the ranch, taught me to serve God and love the land. My husband, Mark, is the kind of person who sees the potential in other people, even when they cannot. His generosity of spirit is limitless. In every possible way, he encourages my journey. He is my first and best editor, my sounding board to work out ideas, and my greatest supporter. I would not be who I am without him.

This book is dedicated to the memory of Elise "Eliza" Rosalia Sternhjem Scheel Haarby Christensen, Maren "Mary" Frederikke Pettersen Christensen, Dorthea Christiane Tranum Christensen, and Anna Sophie Henriksen Wessel-Brown—the women who made C. C. A.'s story possible.

CHAPTER ONE

Journey of a Visionary

The Life and Work of C. C. A. Christensen

Braving snow and winds on a cold February night in 1880, Utah Territory families flocked to the Ogden Fourth Ward schoolhouse to see a presentation of the Mormon Panorama by Carl Christian Anton (C. C. A.) Christensen. Reports in the *Deseret News* and the *Woman's Exponent* lauded Christensen's recent presentations in Salt Lake City and encouraged all to attend.[1] As the Ogden crowd settled onto wooden benches, filling the schoolhouse to capacity, a middle-aged man with friendly blue eyes and a white beard stepped to the podium. Behind him, his six-foot-tall painting of Joseph Smith in the sacred grove stretched ten feet wide between two canvas scrolls wrapped around wooden dowels. The image was lit theatrically by lanterns placed on the floor in front.

In his singsong Danish accent, Christensen began, "This scene represents the first vision of Joseph Smith, the Prophet. He was at that time but a boy of between 14 and 15 years of age."[2] Christensen described Joseph Smith's experience and then led the audience in a hymn as assistants turned the dowels, revealing the next image. The spectators listened in "breathless silence" while scenes of persecution against the Mormons were displayed and explained in detail: Smith tarred and feathered, families forced to flee from burning homes in the night, Smith and his brother Hyrum murdered by a mob, Latter-day Saint children shot and killed at Haun's Mill.[3] Christensen presented the show three more times to packed houses over the next few days in Ogden. He returned in the fall, with two newly painted scenes stitched to the giant scroll, and again drew large crowds for days.[4]

Evenings like these occurred throughout Latter-day Saint cities and settlements in Utah, Wyoming, and Idaho in the 1880s and 1890s. Christensen captured the Mormon imagination with his presentations. He was one of the few formally trained artists among the Latter-day Saints at the time, and he used his skill to great effect. With the Mormon Panorama, he became a painter, historian, and entertainer all in one. Local newspapers excitedly announced his wintertime visits. Handbills recommending the Mormon Panorama were endorsed by Church President John Taylor, First Presidency member Joseph Fielding Smith, and other leaders of The Church of Jesus Christ of Latter-day Saints.[5]

As a form of both instructive and visual entertainment, panoramas were a cinematic sensation in America. Christensen was one of several Latter-day Saint entrepreneurs who produced traveling presentations of a historical lecture with a large painted backdrop. From the late 1840s through the 1880s, Philo Dibble lectured in front of painted scenes of Church history, along with the plaster death masks of Joseph and Hyrum Smith and other relics.[6] In the 1840s, American artists produced dozens of panoramas and showed them throughout many major cities.[7] Dibble was likely inspired by the booming panorama industry in America, which was centered in St. Louis, just 200 miles south of where he lived in Nauvoo.[8] After the Saints settled in Utah, other members, including Reuben Kirkham, Alfred Lambourne, and William Armitage, painted and exhibited panoramas.[9]

Aside from being known for his panorama lectures, Christensen's fame grew during these decades as the Church hired him to paint murals in temples and as the Deseret Sunday School Union distributed copies of his Book of Mormon paintings throughout the region. For many Church members at the time, Christensen's paintings were the first and only images they saw of the Book of Mormon and of Church history. By the end of the nineteenth century, C. C. A. Christensen was among the most famous living illustrators of Latter-day Saint belief and experience. Not only was Christensen well known, but he was influential in shaping Mormon thought with his art and writing. His paintings helped form a sense of cohesive Latter-day Saint identity.

And yet, even while Latter-day Saint culture and thought today are deeply influenced by Christensen's work, members of the Church are now largely unfamiliar with him or his artworks. The recent renovations of the Manti Utah Temple offer a case in point. When leaders of the Church announced in early 2021 that the renovation plan called for removing the temple's interior murals, the public responded with dismay. The community outcry focused on preserving the mural painted by Minerva Teichert in the 1940s. Rallies, news articles, and petitions urged Church leaders to protect Teichert's artwork.[10] By contrast, the public discussion and media coverage largely ignored Christensen's much older mural from 1886, even as the conversation focused on the importance of maintaining artifacts from Church history. Even after the Church revised the plan and retained the murals, when the refurbished Manti Temple reopened in 2024, Teichert's mural continued to receive much more attention than Christensen's.[11]

As the Manti Temple episode illustrates, C. C. A. Christensen and many other nineteenth-century Latter-day Saint artists are largely forgotten. In part, this unawareness derives from mid-twentieth-century programs and commissions by the Church Correlation Department, which in some ways overshadowed earlier artistic production. In fact, Teichert's legacy lapsed too until the late 1990s, when the diligent efforts of art historians and Teichert's descendants recovered her story and presented it to a new generation.[12] Christensen's life and work, on the other hand, have received very little scholarly or popular attention. In a curious reversal, Teichert's art (mostly overlooked by the Church during her lifetime) is now ubiquitous in Church media, while Christensen's art (lauded and institutionally supported in his day) now rarely appears in Church publications.

Although Church correlation may partly explain the decline of Christensen's fame, other factors are at play. Two of Christensen's largest projects were lost to the public for decades—rolled up and stored in the attics of descendants. Church historians only found the *Untitled [Lamanite/Huntington Panorama]*, for instance, in 2010 and did not make images of it public until 2019. Still, many members of the Church are not familiar with the Christensen works that did remain available. The Church's Gospel Art catalog includes just three of his works, all showing pioneers on their trek to the American West.[13] Only four exhibitions have focused attention on Christensen: at the Whitney Museum of American Art in New York in 1970, the Museum of Church History and Art in 1984,[14] and the Brigham Young University Museum of Art in 2004 and 2015.

Art historians, like museums, have given scant attention to Christensen. The most recent publications devoted solely to Christensen are both from 1984: the exhibition catalog, *C. C. A. Christensen: 1831–1912: Mormon Immigrant Artist* by Richard L. Jensen and Richard G. Oman, and Jørgen W. Schmidt's *C. C. A. Christensen. Dansk-americansk maler, digter, samfundsrevser og missionaer* (Danish-American painter, poet, social reformer and missionary). The only other two are William Mulder's 1947 *"Man Kalder Mig Digter": C. C. A. Christensen, Poet of the Scandinavian Scene in Early Utah* and John Hansen's 1921 Danish anthology *Mindeudgave: C. C. A. Christensen: Poetiske Arbejder Artikler og Afhandlinger; tilligemed hans Levnedsløb* (Commemorative edition: C. C. A. Christensen: Poetic Works Articles and Treatises; also His Life).

Christensen's work and influence demand more in-depth scholarly analysis. Christensen was the most prolific painter of Latter-day Saint history and scripture in the nineteenth century. Apart from his visual art production, Christensen established himself as a poet, missionary, farmer, city councilman, political activist, teacher, editor of a newspaper, assistant in the Church Historian's Office, and outspoken essayist on theology, art, politics, city planning, and women's suffrage. Christensen's Protestant upbringing and art education in Denmark, combined with his experience as an American pioneer and early Mormon settler in Utah, uniquely positioned him to bring European training and American expansion ideology to Mormon thought and visual culture. Both Christensen's art and writing responded to and impacted the development of Latter-day Saint thought and culture in nineteenth-century Utah.

In recent years, a few scholars—notably Julie Allen, Paul Anderson, Heather Belnap, Noel Carmack, Ashlee Whitaker Evans, David Grua, Steven Harper, Laura Hurtado, Devan Jensen, Richard Jensen, Richard Oman, Nathan Rees, Jørgen Schmidt, and James Swensen—have begun to re-evaluate Christiansen's art and the role he played in shaping Mormon thought and visual culture in the context of larger studies. However, scholarly treatments of his art tend to focus on the subject matter of his paintings, using them as a springboard to discuss moments in Church history or scripture rather than talking about the paintings themselves. Few studies recognize the role his style, symbolism, and composition play in creating meaning in his art. His paintings also have not received the attention they deserve as historical documents. An art historical analysis allows us to appreciate overlooked elements of his art and to see how his work reflected and even shaped the culture and beliefs of nineteenth-century Latter-day Saints in ways that remain today.

This book seeks to contribute to the growing interest in Christensen's legacy and his influence on Mormon thought and religious art. It offers a thorough and sustained examination of his written and visual work in conversation with each other. This study provides a detailed art historical analysis of Christensen's paintings, including how he used style, symbolism, and composition in sophisticated ways to create meaning in his art that echoed and affected Mormon thought. This analysis re-evaluates Christensen's role in the development of American art and in the formation of Mormon memory and self-identity. Recognizing that his art and writing are inseparable from his lived experience, it draws on his biography to reveal Christensen's complex relationship with the symbol of wilderness and how the American frontier represented ideas about political and religious liberty (explored further in chapter two), his ability to blend European, American, and distinctly Latter-day Saint ideologies and iconographies (addressed in chapter three), and his passionate dedication to both his Scandinavian heritage and the Zion community he envisioned in America (for more, see chapter four). Finally, the bibliographic essay details Christensen's artistic oeuvre and writings and considers their reception.

Christensen was a visionary not only in the sense of being among the first artists to visualize Mormon experience and scripture, but also in the sense that he built his life (often at great personal cost) around an idea of what the future could be. He believed he had a role to play in making the dream of Zion a reality. He consecrated his life to that ideal and sought to instill the vision in others through his painting, public presentations, teaching, writing, community building, missionary work, and Church service.

Early Life in Denmark

Christensen was both a wide-eyed dreamer and a disciplined hard worker. He was born to Mads and Dorthea Christiane Tranum Christensen in Copenhagen, Denmark, on November 28, 1831. The family lived humbly, with Mads's alcoholism exacerbating their financial struggles. After failing at inn ownership, Mads worked in a factory while Dorthea started a shop, took in laundry, and cleaned homes. Although still young himself, as the oldest child, C. C. A. often had to take his baby brother across town to be nursed by his mother. Later, Christensen reflected in his first diary book, "The cleaning of the house, as well as other necessary chores, I did as well as I could, and I can say, that I put forth an effort, so that everything should be all right when my mother came home in the evening."[15] This strong sense of duty and responsibility would remain with him. From his mother, he also inherited a creative, visionary approach to life. She taught him to make toys and decorations using paper and scissors.[16] She also occasionally took him to a Baptist church and shared her spiritual temperament with her children. Christensen recorded that Dorthea had at least two dreams about his future success when he was just a toddler.[17]

Despite the family's efforts, once Christensen's third younger brother came along, the family could no longer support all the children. At eleven years old, C. C. A. was placed in *Kongelige Opfostringhus* (Royal Orphanage), a poor house boarding school. There he spent half his time in trade school, where he first learned toy-making and then served as an apprentice to carpenter F. C. Möller. One Christmas, he decorated the orphanage tree with the cut paper designs learned from his mother. His skill impressed a wealthy widow, Anne Sophie Henriksen Wessel-Brown, and she arranged to send him to *Det Kongelige Danske Kunstakademi* (The Royal Danish Academy of Fine Arts) in the evenings during the winters. By the summer of 1848, Christensen had enrolled full time at the Academy and begun to learn painting as an apprentice to master painter Carl Rosent.[18]

Christensen reached adulthood just as his country entered a new era. In June 1849, shortly before Christensen's eighteenth birthday, Denmark adopted a constitution that allowed unprecedented freedom of religion in the predominantly Lutheran country. Latter-day Saint Church leaders in Utah wasted no time in calling missionaries to Denmark. By the following summer, Elder Erastus Snow and Brother Peter Hansen were preaching in Copenhagen and finding success among members of the Baptist church attended by Christensen's mother. The missionaries baptized Dorthea in August 1850. Christensen had not been particularly religious as a youth, but he decided to be baptized on September 26, 1850. He wrote in his diary, "The sky had thus far been clouded, but in the minutes I went down into the waters to be immersed in the watery grave the moon again came out from its hiding place and seemed to be smiling at us and showing us the goodwill of the Lord, and at the same time showing a picture of the change that took place in our souls."[19] Christensen's inclination to see nature as a symbol for spiritual matters would become a theme in his later art and writing.

Christensen prioritized his Church learning and service over his art career training. Although he finished his apprenticeship, passed the final exam, and graduated from the Academy in January 1853, Christensen never took the advanced live-model figure drawing classes that most other students completed. In fact, he applied twice for the elite course (in October 1850 and January 1852) and was rejected by a juried committee both times.[20] Christensen may have seen limits to his potential fine arts career in Europe. This portent, combined with Latter-day Saint teachings about the urgency of escaping from corrupt traditions to prepare for an impending apocalypse, guided Christensen away from the high culture represented by the Academy.[21] Having had some luck but never having had real economic success, Christensen may have felt his options were just as good, if not better, in the rural American West. As a new convert, he wrote, "My prospective success as an artist-painter seemed suddenly to be swallowed up or ruined forever, as we looked for the end of the world in a very few years. I therefore slackened a great deal in my efforts to become an artist, yet I continued attending the art academy till I had served my time as an apprentice and had passed my examination."[22]

In the meantime, Christensen read the Bible, the Book of Mormon (as it was translated into Danish in a weekly pamphlet), and Elder Snow's newspaper for Church members called *Skandinaviens Stjerne* (Scandinavian Star).[23] He helped J. M. Bohn create the first Danish Latter-day Saint hymnbook, which included some of Christensen's own compositions. By 1853, Christensen's mother and two of his brothers had immigrated to Utah, but he stayed behind to serve a Scandinavian mission before joining them. Although his family made it to Salt Lake City, Christensen's mother passed away there in 1855 before he could see her again.

Despite the new Danish law guaranteeing freedom of worship, members of the fledgling Copenhagen Branch experienced persecution and even physical assault.[24] Generations of loyalty to the Danish Lutheran Church made the Danish people skeptical of other religions, particularly one that was seen as so essentially foreign. As historians Reid Neilson and Scott Marianno point out, while joining the Church may have been legal, it also "moved a person outside of the boundaries of Danish respectability."[25] In his first short autobiography in 1853, Christensen remembered that, "From the time of my baptism on I became an object of ridicule and some persecution, even from my former friends, and, being of a sensitive nature, it was sometimes a severe trial to me."[26] Christensen wrote that vigilantes "did all they could to disturb our meetings, yes even to hit some of our brethren in a violent way."[27]

In Norway, the persecution was even worse. There, members of the Church did not fall under the category of "Christian dissenters," and so they did not enjoy the same religious liberties.[28] In March 1854, Norwegian police arrested Christensen and his missionary companion, Carl Christian Nicoli Dorius, and ordered them to stop proselyting. When the pair refused, the authorities jailed them for three weeks.[29] In April 1854, Christensen spent another five days in the same Norwegian cell, this time receiving only bread and water.[30] On another occasion, a menacing mob followed Christensen at night, attacking him with ice and snowballs. In an article published years later in the *Juvenile Instructor*, Christensen recounted the incident as an example of God's protective power when one faithfully stands up to abusive mockery. After repeated pelting and jeers, he turned to face his hecklers and said, "Gentlemen, here I am. What have I done to harm you? If my religion is wrong and yours is right, then I don't think you are taking the right course to convince me of my errors; and if your faith is better than mine, then show it forth in a peaceable manner!"[31]

Christensen filled his diary with detailed daily entries for this first mission. Writing in Gothic Danish with an elegant cursive, he recorded the names of people and places he visited and even commented on the weather. He spent his busy days in meetings and church conferences and painted houses to support himself. On this mission, he also met Danquart Anthon Weggeland, whom he would later partner with on painting commissions in Utah. In his writing, he seems energized and eager, with a good sense of humor. He reveals his attitude in a poem from May 1853:

> Listen, my friends, if you know me;
> Christensen is my good name.
> I am a painter. I speak the language
> Nicely, as in Copenhagen.
> My height is medium, eyes are blue,
> Hair is blond and ears small.
> My nose was placed, very opportunely,
> Between my other senses.[32]

His dry wit appears again in passages such as this one, from November 4, 1853, upon his arrival in Christiania (Oslo), Norway, "After a refreshing sleep we were awakened early in the morning by the cries of the housewife, and thus we had the pleasure, when the man apologized for this disturbance, of congratulating him on the arrival of a new member of the family."[33]

In this early diary, Christensen frequently mentions visiting the Haarby family, including young Elise Rosalia Sternhjem Scheel Haarby. In June 1854, Christensen proposed to Elise with a poem, but her parents had reservations about her joining the Church, and particularly about the practice of polygamy in Utah.[34] Three years later, C. C. A. and Elise, now baptized, finally married at a stop in Liverpool on their way to the United States.[35]

Joining the Saints in Utah

The Christensens arrived in Philadelphia by ship in 1857 and then took the train to Iowa City. From there, they spent their honeymoon pulling handcarts to Salt Lake City. They first lived in Cedar Valley and then in Lehi. Elise gave birth to their first child, Elisa (Eliza) Virginia, in February 1859, and the next month they relocated to nearby Mount Pleasant in Sanpete County. At the end of that year, C. C. A. and Elise received their endowment and sealing ordinances from Church President Brigham Young in Salt Lake City. In 1860, they moved to North Bend (Fairview), where their son Charles John joined the family in 1861. A month later, they moved again, this time back to Mount Pleasant.

Although Christensen had once dreamed of becoming a painter in Europe, he now needed to support his family in a small Utah settlement farming wheat, oats, corn, potatoes, and garden vegetables. Opportunities for skilled painters were scarce, yet Christensen put his artistic training to use in creative ways. In 1862, the Springville theater hired Christensen to paint scenery, giving him enough extra income to buy a cow. His painting at Springville earned him a recommendation from Bernard Snow to President Young in November 1862. Snow noted that "he [Christensen] follows farming at present, but would be very glad to turn his attention to the finer arts if he can get an opening to sustain himself and family by it."[36] Perhaps because of this letter, the next year Christensen obtained work painting the newly constructed theater in Salt Lake City. This job helped pay off his emigration debt. In the summer of 1863, he and Elise welcomed a son, Frederik William. He continued to find occasional artistic jobs—often carpentry or painting houses and signs—in addition to his farming work.[37]

In 1865, with Elise expecting their fourth child, President Young called Christensen on a second mission to Scandinavia and gave him only two weeks' notice to depart. With his characteristic drollery, Christensen later wrote that since he then had "considerable live issue in the form of children, but no dead issue in the shape of money," he had to sell his cows and most of his wheat to buy a yoke of cattle for transport.[38] The journey required a 1,000-mile trek eastward across the plains before reaching riverboats and railways to New York, a transatlantic voyage, and a ship to Copenhagen.

Christensen's second mission journals differ in form and tone from his first. Notably, he began to write in English and included a few small artworks. The earliest journal from this mission begins in Utah with a watercolor sketch of Mt. Nebo and Utah Lake. He started a second journal, also purchased in Salt Lake City and carried with him, several months later. It has five sketches in the back pages: three sketches of Pawnee people, a sketch of men and wagons, and a rough sketch of a horse. It appears that Christensen later made a cleaner and more complete version of these mission journals. The later reproduction begins with details about his mission calling, including a transcription of the letter from Brigham Young that called him to service. A comparison of the field journals and the later journal shows that Christensen made cuts and additions, intending for this copy to be a lasting historical document. A commitment to recording and preserving history remained a driving motivation for him.

In contrast to journals from his first mission, the second mission journal entries are monthly reports, rather than daily logs. In the entries, Christensen often seems bored by the routine. He looks for ways to fill the time, such as doing genealogy work for a fellow Dane back in Utah, visiting museums and historic sites, and taking landscape painting and photography classes. His writing exudes a nostalgia for both Danish and American landscapes and people, and he seems no longer quite at home in either place. To his disappointment, upon his arrival, he found that his father had died a few years earlier. At the same time, Christensen constantly missed and worried about his wife and four children, who suffered illness and financial hardship in Utah during his work abroad. In the first year of his mission, he wrote this poem, which was included in the Danish hymn book:

> Do they miss me at home in the valley?
> Am I mentioned among those I love?
> When the children are lovingly hugged
> And kissed, O! How I wish I were near!
> When early they kneel for prayer
> And angels smile at the little ones

Do anyone's thoughts dwell
On the one who now must be lonely?[39]

Christensen arrived home in Utah in August 1868 with Elise's parents in tow. Although her mother, Andrea Larsen Haarby, was baptized, her stepfather, Niels Shaug Haarby, was not. The couple settled close to the Christensens in Mount Pleasant. Perhaps the Haarbys had experienced a change of heart about the practice of plural marriage. Or, if not, Christensen confirmed their worst fears when he took Maren "Mary" Frederikke Pettersen as his second wife. A twenty-three-year-old woman from Norway, Mary had joined Christensen's traveling company in Europe before continuing to the United States in a different ship. Christensen and Mary married in the Salt Lake City endowment house on November 30, 1868.[40] With resources scarce, he took a job working on the Union Pacific railroad and lived in the railroad camp for eight weeks that winter.[41]

In 1870, the household(s) moved to Ephraim, where Elise and Mary lived in houses next door to each other on Main Street. Mary gave birth to her first child, Mary Ann, in June. The children kept coming fast: a total of seven to each wife. Niels Erastus was born to Elise in 1870, Julia Eleanora to Mary in 1871, Canute Ephraim to Elise in 1872, Caroline Maria (who lived four months) to Mary in 1873, Teckla Pauline to Elise in 1874, John Carlos to Mary in 1875, George Parley Brigham to Mary in 1877, Joseph Anthony (who lived seven months) to Mary in 1880, and Hyrum Moroni to Mary in 1882. Descendants of the family recall that the children all considered each other brothers and sisters. The two houses shared a root cellar, barns, and livestock. As was common practice among polygamous families in Sanpete County, Elise's children and grandchildren referred to Christensen's second wife as "Aunt Mary."[42]

In the second half of the 1870s, Christensen, Elise, and at least some of their children homesteaded in Manasseh, just a few miles from Ephraim. Elise and the children appear to have mostly lived alone in a small log cabin while Christensen traveled for work and back and forth to town.[43] Some of Elise's children seem to have stayed in Ephraim with Mary so they could attend school. While Christensen was away in February 1880, Elise wrote to him reporting that her children were recovering from colds and commenting that "maybe Mary has or will write you when she is well enough. I hear she has had a boy," before remarking on the unusually cold weather, food ration concerns, low production of milk and eggs from their livestock, and directions to buy cotton fabric for the children's clothes.[44]

During these busy domestic years, Christensen painted *Weighing the Baby* (Fig. 1.1). It is the third known painting by Christensen after an earlier portrait of his own children (Eliza and Charles) and a painting of an emigrant ship completed during his second mission. *Weighing the Baby* depicts the John Frederick Ferdinand Dorius family, close friends from Denmark now settled in Ephraim. Christensen, John F. F. Dorius, and his brother Carl C. N. Dorius had been missionary companions in the 1850s and immigrated to Utah together. Christensen completed the scene in the style of a small cabinet painting, indicating it was likely meant to be viewed only by family and close friends. Clearly inspired by genre scenes of the Northern European tradition, there are echoes of a lively Jan Steen domestic interior but played out through the Mormon experience. It presents a vignette of a tidy and well-ordered polygamous home.[45] One wife recovers in bed after

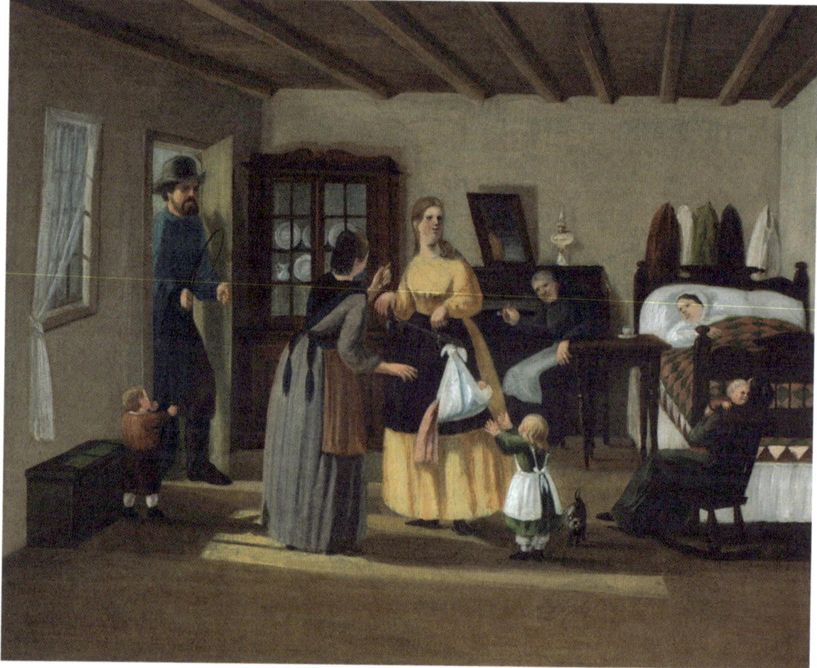

Figure 1.1 C. C. A. Christensen, *Weighing the Baby*, 1872, oil on canvas, 8 × 10 inches, Springville Museum of Art, gift from Diane and Sam Stewart, Salt Lake City.

the birth of a baby. The other wife stands in the center of the room with the midwife as they check the baby's weight. Two other women and three more children fill the space. John F. F. Dorius stands at the threshold of interior and exterior space and looks on proudly. Christensen likely drew on his own experiences with a growing family when he undertook this painting.

Weighing the Baby is characteristic of Christensen's art. It showcases his clever sense of humor by positioning the man of the house almost as an afterthought, perpetually standing outside the enclosed circle of women and children. The piece also exhibits an attention to detail that became a hallmark of Christensen's artwork. Although it is a small painting, Christensen took care to lovingly recreate the space and objects, including the weighing mechanism, a quilt neatly laid over the bed, an elegant wood and glass cabinet displaying crockery, a rocking chair for tending babies, a fireplace where the grandmother keeps warm, exposed wooden beams on the ceiling, a rectangle of light that falls from the window across the floor, and even the family kitten.

To support the family during the 1870s, Christensen took odd jobs painting window blinds, coffins, and grave markers.[46] Then, in 1875, he embarked on a string of projects depicting Latter-day Saint doctrine and history: a painted scroll with scenes from the Bible and Book of Mormon, a large panorama illustrating the history of the early Latter-day Saints in the United States, and a smaller history series.

First, Dimick Huntington commissioned Christensen to paint a twenty-two-foot-long vertical scroll comprised of eleven scenes, known today as the *Untitled [Lamanite/Huntington] Panorama*. Huntington and his missionary companion, George Washington Hill, used this scroll as a visual aid in their preaching to Utes and Shoshone in Utah Territory.[47] It begins with Adam and Eve in the Garden of Eden, and then moves through important events for God's people in both the Old and New Worlds, concluding with Joseph Smith receiving plates of scripture from Moroni.[48]

Perhaps inspired by the Huntington commission, Christensen began work on his Mormon Panorama in 1877 or 1878. This much larger scroll wound horizontally and eventually included twenty-three images. With each painted canvas stitched to the previous one, Christensen added scenes until about 1890. The scenes visualize moments from early Latter-day Saint history, beginning in New York with Joseph Smith, before tracing the Saints' movement to Missouri, then Ohio, then Illinois, and finally Utah. Each scene details episodes of persecution alongside travels through the

American wilderness. The Mormon Panorama profoundly influenced the way members of the Church recalled their early history. In the 1870s and 1880s, the generation of Latter-day Saints who had first come across the plains and settled in the Great Basin was dying out. Christensen noticed this change and the need to teach the younger generation about the persecution that forced their parents west. In 1879, he wrote in *Bikuben* (a Utah newspaper for Danish immigrants), "The old generation who bore the burdens of the day in the persecutions in Ohio, Missouri, and Illinois will no longer be with us a few years hence. History will preserve much, but art alone can make the narrative of the suffering of the Saints comprehensible for posterity."[49] Presentations of his Mormon Panorama paintings, along with a prepared lecture to explain the visuals, were his way of addressing this problem. In doing so, Christensen leaned into a persecution narrative that defined Latter-day Saint identity and experience.

Christensen only mentioned traveling with the Mormon Panorama once, in December 1889, in his journals, but he did show the panorama publicly many times.[50] As early as 1879, the *Deseret News* described a public showing of the panorama.[51] In 1883, the same newspaper reported that Christensen showed the panorama while he lectured on Church history, but the author felt that the experience would be improved if Christensen found someone "to travel with him who could speak the English language more clearly and effectively."[52] Christensen's son Charles soon took over the lecture responsibilities. Christensen and Charles spent many winters, when farm work was slow, traveling through Latter-day Saint settlements in Utah, Wyoming, and Idaho to present the panorama and lecture. In this way, they raised some money for the large family.

Christensen's local renown as a painter led Church leaders to hire him, along with Weggeland, in 1881 to paint murals in the St. George Temple.[53] In 1886, Church leaders again hired Christensen, this time to paint an endowment room mural in the Manti Temple, just a few miles from his home in Ephraim. He painted the periods of creation directly into the plaster of the walls. The cycle begins on the front left of the room, with the separation of night and day visualized with clouds and shadows. Moving to the right, a volcano erupts as the seas and earth are parted. Along the side wall, Christensen presents a variety of lush vegetation, including hollyhocks, roses, and Lombardy poplars, all plants familiar to nineteenth-century Utah Saints. The creation of animals starts with Mesozoic creatures, then moves to fowls, then land animals, and finally marine creatures (Fig. 1.2).

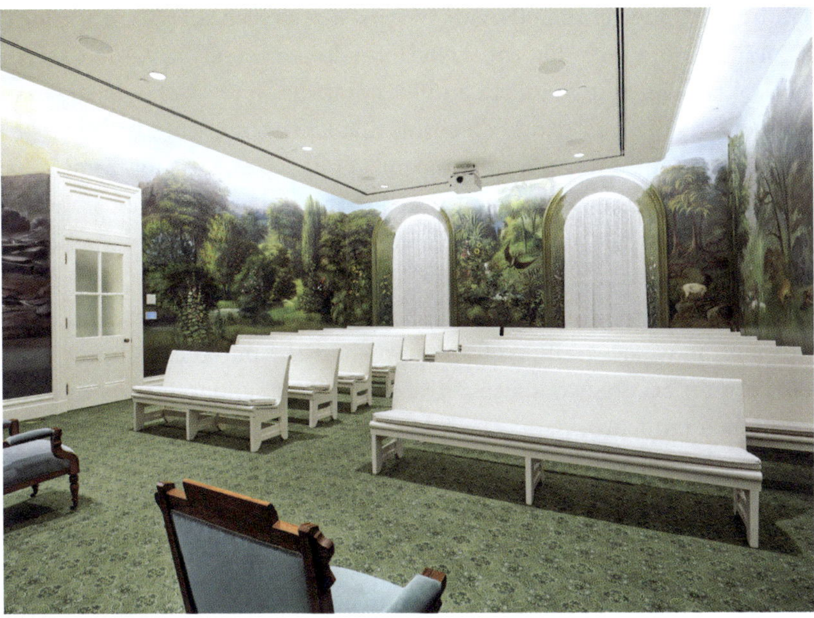

Figure 1.2 C. C. A. Christensen, Detail from creation room, c. 1886–1887, oil on gesso, 16 feet high, Manti Temple, © By Intellectual Reserve, Inc.

Scholars have noticed clear similarities between Christensen's Mesozoic animals and Édouard Riou's illustrations in Louis Figuier's *La Terre Avant Le Deluge* (The Earth Before The Flood) of 1863, which was published in English in 1865.[54] Figuier's lengthy book aimed to make the burgeoning field of natural history accessible to the public with engravings of fossils, illustrations of landscapes and animals, diagrams of volcanoes and tectonic plates, maps, and charts. Indeed, at the time, it was the only printed source to illustrate the Earth's early geography, flora, and fauna for a general audience.[55] An instant classic, *La Terre Avant Le Deluge* "set the standard for the emergent History of Life genre."[56] Its initial printing in France sold out immediately, and it quickly went through several editions and additional printings. The popular work fit nicely with Christensen's project because it showed the development of various plant and animal species over time. The temple murals similarly display a sense of deep time ordered into discrete periods. The erupting volcano draws on several of Riou's illustrations, combining the volcanic cone and billowing cloud of ash in "Fig. 9.—Section of a volcano in action," the spray of lava and rock in "Fig. 10.—Existing crater of Vesuvius," and the distinctive zig-zags of lightning bolts in "XII.—Ideal landscape of the Permian Period."[57] Christensen's scene of prehistoric life is a composite of Riou's "Fig. 83—Labyrinthodon restored," "XV.—Ideal scene of the Lias with Ichthyosaurus and Plesiosaurus," and "XVI.—Ideal Landscape of the Liassic Period."[58] It seems that Christensen, always interested in historical accuracy, looked to the images in this volume for inspiration.

Christensen likely also used printed sources to help him conceptualize his large mammals and fowls. He would not have seen savanna beasts, jungle birds, or sea creatures in Utah. Yet, he skillfully portrayed an elephant mother playing with her baby, colorful birds dotting the trees, and a line of spouting whales trailing off in the corner. The mural exudes not just a concern for accuracy but also a love for God's creations and joy in being embodied in the world.

In the late 1880s, Christensen painted several additional scenes of Church history. These undated pieces are comparable in style to his *Sugar Creek* and *Defense of Nauvoo in September 1846*, which he did in 1885–1886. These paintings all have similar titles, listing both a place and a date across the lower canvas: *Crossing the Mississippi Feb: 1846*; *Liberty Jail Clay Co., Mo.; B. Y. Calling Volunteers for the Mormon Battalion*; *Mormon Battalion Ball, July 1846*; *Crossing the Missouri River*; *Winter Quarters 1846–1847*. As the 1880s drew to a close, Christensen had established himself as a significant contributor to the Church's visual imagery, a role that enabled him to shape how the Saints imagined both their past and the scriptural narratives they celebrated.

A Third Mission

In 1887, Church leaders called Christensen to Scandinavia as a missionary for a third time. He served in Denmark from August 1887 to July 1889. Almost as soon as he arrived in Copenhagen, he had lithographs made from his painting *The Restoration of the Aaronic Priesthood*. The scene takes place in a forest and shows John the Baptist giving the priesthood to Joseph Smith and Oliver Cowdery, depicting an event that occurred sixty years earlier in 1829. Having now had some financial success with art, Christensen made these lithographs to raise additional funds. He sent 1,500 of the prints home to Utah for his family to sell. He also gave fifty copies to Brother Fjeldsted in his mission "to assist him in his expenditures" and another fifty to the leader of the mission, President Flygare, "to aid other brethren with."[59]

During this mission, Christensen once again stayed busy. He took advantage of his time in Europe to frequent museums and exhibitions.[60] In September 1888, at Frederiksborg Castle, he saw a series on the life of Christ painted by his former Academy classmate, Carl Bloch. In addition, he took over as editor of the *Skandinaviens Stjerne*. He frequently published his own writings in the semi-monthly paper. He also made corrections to the Danish hymnal.

Christensen's journal entries from this mission are sporadic and short. He sometimes felt that nothing much was happening, and his mood seemed weary. He recorded several illnesses and some challenging relationships with other missionaries (especially one man who feared Christensen would usurp his Danish translating duties). Christensen continued to worry about his family in Utah, particularly his son Niels Erastus, age nineteen, who was living away from home. Christensen feared Niels had fallen in with a bad crowd. He wrote one entry as a sort of psalm, pleading for his son. Then, in a letter home in September 1888, Christensen asked,

> Could you arrange that Frederik and Charles take the 'Panorama' to some of the northern settlements or up to a place that is near his [Niels's] residence, and let him meet them there and get him in on the right track. Sometimes I think with sadness that it is my fault that he got on the wrong track because I was not tolerant enough towards him, but it was from fear that his example would infect my other children that I was so hard on him, though not harder than towards his older brothers.[61]

The plan seems to have worked, as a few months later Christensen wrote to Niels, "My dear son! It is with much satisfaction, that I have learned, that you have commenced going to the Academy School, and, I hope, that you will continue as long as ordinary circumstances will allow you to do so, for you can not possibly spend your time and means to better advantage."[62]

Sadly, Christensen's joy was short-lived. Five months later, he received the devastating news that Niels had died in a logging accident. His journal entry on this sorrowful event captures much of Christensen's sensibilities—he is nostalgic, attentive, faithful, hopeful, and poetic, even in despair.

> On the 4th I arose at four o'clock a.m. and took a long walk out in the country and into the woods, and I enjoyed this my lonely trip immensely, as I, in my mind, called back many a boyish act and incident from these

> familiar scenes, that seemed exactly as the[y] were 40 years ago. I also flung my thoughts across the mighty deep, a branch of which, washes the lovely shores of Seeland, on which the capital of Denmark is situated, but my soul was yet in ignorance of the sad calamity that had visited my beloved far-off home, but a few days previous. On the 13th the mail brought me three letters from home, all informing me of the Death of my beloved son Niels Erastus. He met with his death, while working at brother Terry's sawmill, about 13 miles East from Fairview. He was engaged in taking the lumber away from the saw, and while thus taking the last board away from the saw, before going to take dinner, the saw, which was in motion, struck a knot, and caused that end of the board, of which Erastus had hold, to fly up and strike him on the left side of the neck, with such force, that he died instantly; the neck being broken. It seems, that great symphaty [*sic*] was shown to my bereaved family in this trying hour, by many of the people of Ephraim, and through the papers, but I have not yet learned that the President of the Stake, Canute Petersen or his councilor, Henry Beal, who both live in the same street, where my family lives, have visited them or in any other way shown their sympaty [*sic*] for the sufferers or a regard for the father, who is abroad on a mission. By letters from home, I learn, that the comforting influence of the holy spirit, has given my wife, mother of the deceased, strength to bear up under these trying circumstances, with a remarkable degree of fortitude. Also to me, has the Lord been merciful in this respect, and I feel reconciled to what has happened, believing that a kind of Providence has done all for the best of all parties concerned.[63]

Christensen's decision to begin the journal's July entry by recounting a lovely, nostalgic walk in the Danish countryside adds a startling poignancy to the announcement of his son's death. Landscapes, and especially landscapes connected to history and important moments, dominated Christensen's thoughts and art throughout his life. Pain pervades his comment that the stake presidency has not visited his family or written to him (Christensen emphasizes the men's failure by mentioning they live on his family's street). He knows that transatlantic communication is slow, and he hints that he may be jumping to conclusions, but in this moment of grief, he allows himself to do so anyway. He is serving a mission away from his family for a third time, after much personal and financial sacrifice and hardship. He expects some help from the community—if not for him, then at least for his wives and children. Still, ever faithful, by the end of the entry, Christensen can confess his trust in God, and he witnesses that he felt comforted by the Spirit.

Christensen's third and final mission encapsulates much of his character. Art and faith, which he often combined, drove his life. Following the death of his son, however, Christensen longed to return to Utah even though he knew the homecoming would likely result in persecution for polygamy.

Later Years

After waiting several months for his replacement, Christensen finally requested immediate release from the Scandinavian mission. In the fall of 1889, he stopped in Liverpool on his way to New York, then took a train to Virginia. In a dramatic shift from his first frontier crossing by handcart in 1857, this time he rode the transcontinental railroad all the way to the Rocky Mountains. Christensen arrived home just in time for the birthday he and Niels shared on November 28, now a bittersweet occasion.

The railroad and loss of a son were not the only major changes Christensen faced. Federal authorities greeted Christensen almost instantly in Utah with a warrant for his arrest for unlawful cohabitation. Indeed, increased legal prosecution of polygamy may have been the reason Christensen was sent away on this mission. He seemed to know what awaited him in Utah when he wrote to Elise from Europe, "Please do not think about the unpleasant welcome waiting for me, but let it rest and give it over to the hands of the Lord. I do not fear for that trial as much as some do, because I have been in prison before, though not as bad as what is waiting for me now."[64] He was released on bond while he awaited trial.

In the meantime, he began work on a series of paintings based on the Book of Mormon, competing for a prize offered by the Deseret Sunday School Union. In 1890, his hometown displayed the paintings in the Ephraim Tabernacle.[65] The Deseret Sunday School Union selected Christensen's ten Book of Mormon paintings for the prize of $20 each (along with two by other artists), and the Church printed the images as lithographs in the *Juvenile Instructor* in 1891. Christensen's Book of Mormon series brings European iconography and style to bear on new scripture in a new world. His approach draws on Old-World academic history painting, including an emphasis on naturalism and a preoccupation with historical detail. But Christensen combined European tropes with innovative and conspicuous Latter-day Saint symbolism. These widely viewed pictures were among just a handful of Book of Mormon images available to the public until the 1950s. Scholars are only beginning to understand the full weight of their importance in delineating Latter-day Saint iconography and belief.

Christensen's polygamy trial dragged on until his eventual conviction in the First District Court of Provo. But he appealed the case on a matter of legal process, and in 1891, the Utah Territorial Supreme Court found him not guilty.[66] Of course, the Manifesto of 1890 had been issued by this time, and prosecution for unlawful cohabitation was waning.

Around this time, Christensen began to focus more on his writing. He regularly wrote articles and letters to the editor for *Bikuben* (The Beehive). His writing also appeared in *Juvenile Instructor*, *Morgenstjernen* (Morning Star), *Deseret Evening News*, and *The Ephraim Enterprise*. His contributions covered diverse topics including fine art, water rights and use, economic development of the region, community improvements and public architecture, politics, and history. In addition, he regularly published original poems.

Christensen became an outspoken advocate for community development and political principles. In his frequent letters to the editor of *Bikuben* about water rights, he often bemoaned the lack of care for the Ephraim cemetery, in the form of little landscaping and no water allocation. He also recommended that his fellow townspeople visit Logan and Salt Lake City to see the more refined architecture there and to bring those styles to the Sanpete Valley. His concerns extended to the economic development of the region as well, and he advocated for better labor wages. He assisted with political polling in Ephraim and spoke in the Assembly Hall about the principles of republicanism.[67]

During his last decades, Christensen maintained his determination to stay busy and productive within his community. In addition to his writing, from 1893–1894, he taught a drawing class at the Sanpete Stake Academy (renamed Snow College). He served as a patriarch and helped organize Scandinavian memorials and gatherings. Starting in 1901, he helped compile a history of the Scandinavian Mission alongside Assistant Church Historian Andrew Jenson. Despite his many endeavors, in the 1890s, Christensen came to feel overlooked as a part of the older generation. His zeal and willingness to serve had not diminished, though, and he did not like to feel sidelined. At the annual Scandinavian celebration in June 1894, he recited in

Danish an allegorical poem he wrote about once-useful items now grown old and thrown into a junk pile. It begins,

> If I were H. C. Andersen,[68] I would write,
> How something big can finally become nothing.
> But now it's another one that is writing,
> And he's never been big, and this won't be either.
>
> I thought about what I saw and heard,
> When I wasn't thinking about where the road led me,
> I passed by a foundry and saw a pile of junk
> And I thought, so it goes when you get worn and old.[69]

In 1899, the family suffered another misfortune when Mary's daughter Julia died in childbirth. Christensen's beloved first wife, Elise, passed in May 1910. Her son Frederik died in May 1912. At the time of his own death in July 1912, Christensen left behind Mary (his second wife), ten children, thirty-nine grandchildren, and two great-grandchildren. He had lived a life consecrated to his beliefs. Christensen lived during a time of enormous change in both Scandinavia and the United States. Enthusiasm for the imminent millennium drew Christensen to the Church just before his nineteenth birthday. Indeed, his zeal to prepare for the end times made him put aside his formal canvas painting for decades. Political and social revolutions—a new constitution in Denmark and large-scale emigration from Scandinavia—heightened the feeling of accelerating change in the world around him. Religious convictions called Christensen to give up career opportunities in Europe to live the life of a poor farmer in Utah.

As the years went by, Christensen's view shifted to more long-term goals. He witnessed the completion of the transcontinental railroad in 1869 and the famed closing of the American frontier in the 1890s. He experienced the turn of the twentieth century. He saw loved ones pass away. He watched first-generation convert immigrants, such as himself, growing old. Toward the end of the nineteenth century, Christensen turned his focus to building community, teaching the younger generation, and recording history. He kept meticulous journals, sometimes even rewriting them later to add more details. He helped write the history of the Scandinavian mission, and he wrote for Danish publications in Utah. He taught Danish at Sanpete Academy. And he returned to canvas painting as a way of documenting the experiences of the early Saints.

Christensen envisioned a glorious Zion community, and he threw himself into the work of building it. Christensen never abandoned his Danish heritage but instead worked throughout his life and through his art to blend European, American, and Latter-day Saint ideologies. Christensen used painting as a vehicle to express political and religious ideas. His art both reflected and influenced the culture and beliefs of nineteenth-century Utah. Through art, writing, poetry, and public lectures to the communities of Utah in the nineteenth century, Christensen shaped Latter-day Saint identity.

CHAPTER TWO

Israelite Wilderness and American Frontier

Exile and Restoration in the Panoramas

Beginning in 1871, Christensen distinguished himself as one of the first painters of the Restoration. Very little fine art painting and essentially no religiously themed painting exists from the initial forty years of The Church of Jesus Christ of Latter-day Saints, from 1830 to 1870. Then, the Latter-day Saint painters of the late nineteenth century primarily focused on landscapes. In 1890, Church leaders sent four members—John Hafen, Lorus Pratt, John B. Fairbanks, and Edwin Evans—to Académie Julian in Paris for art training.[1] Upon their return, these men used the skills learned to decorate the Salt Lake Temple and to produce many landscape paintings. Other artists—such as George Ottinger, James T. Harwood, Alfred Lambourne, Reuben Kirkham, and William Armitage—also painted landscapes and, occasionally, scenes from Church history. At the same time, Christensen painted landscape murals in the Latter-day Saint temples in Manti and St. George and incorporated forests into many of his artworks. It is perhaps not surprising that landscape was a popular genre for early Latter-day Saint artists; after all, the religion began with a vision of the divine in a grove of trees. But the Saints were likely influenced by contemporary American art trends outside of Utah, which exulted in American wilderness.

Beginning in the 1820s, American artists such as Thomas Cole, Frederick Edwin Church, and Asher B. Durand focused on nature in their art. Their work was foundational to the Hudson River School art movement and characterized by a meditative mood and the predominance of landscape over figures and man-made structures. Many Hudson River School paintings emphasize the fleeting nature of human life compared to the deep time of nature. Coles's *Interior of the Colosseum, Rome* (1832), for instance, shows the stone structure crumbling under the elements and being reclaimed by vegetation.[2] In this work and others, there is a sense of the cyclical character of wilderness. Many American artists who worked in this style traveled to Europe and were influenced by earlier English artists like John Constable and J. M. W. Turner, who privileged emotive landscapes. In their work, nature helps tell the story. The Hudson River School artists, too, were not merely documenting nature but using it symbolically, often to make a statement against industrialization and deforestation. This attention to landscape and its use as a symbol continued into the later nineteenth century, when Albert Bierstadt produced massive, idealized views of the American West.

In the European and American imagination, the symbolic function of wilderness is often fluid—sometimes representing evil, exile, and struggle, and other times representing righteousness, chosenness, and providence. In the foreboding opening line of his *Divine Comedy*, Dante Alighieri wrote that he found himself in a *selva oscura* or "dark wood."[3] The *selva oscura* embodies ideas about Christian guilt, alienation from God, and the spiritual disorientation of having lost the right way.[4] Yet, scholar Robert Pogue Harrison notes that Dante also represents the Garden of Eden as a dense, ancient woodland called the *selva antica*.[5] In Christian scripture and thought, wilderness is invoked as both a place of hardship and degeneration and a place of divine protection and redemption. According to European Christian traditions, the fall of Adam changed what was a sylvan earthly paradise into a fearful forest populated by wild beasts.[6] Yet, God's covenant people might still find providence in the forest as they work toward the ultimate promise of restoration. According to historian Perry Miller, the Englishmen who settled America were largely driven by a theology based on this conception of the dual role of wilderness. In that regard, America was understood as a hidden wilderness preserved by God for a special moment of redemption. Miller cites English Anglican cleric Samuel Purchas, who, in 1625, described the Virginia colony carved out of the American wilderness as the Christian errand of Englishmen to redeem the curse on both man and earth.[7] The wilderness is dangerous but full of possibility, and shot through with religious significance. It is the site of original sin and of eventual redemption.

This understanding of the dual character of wilderness is apparent in Latter-day Saint thought. As Latter-day Saint scholar Hugh Nibley observed in his classic treatment on the Book of Mormon, "The desert [wilderness] has two faces; it is a place both of death and of refuge, of defeat and victory, a grim coming-down from Eden and yet a sure escape from the wicked world; the asylum alike of the righteous and the rascal."[8] Early translators of the Bible used the word wilderness to denote undeveloped land, which in the climate of the ancient Near East often meant desert.[9] But for nineteenth-century Americans living in the Northeast, the idea of wilderness applied almost exclusively to forests. The Book of Mormon follows American thought on this: For the Nephites, the wilderness of the promised land largely suggests forest.[10]

The dual nature of wilderness appears in Christensen's painted forests. Like the Hudson River School artists, Christensen used landscape to visually convey a story, mood, or message. From jagged branches symbolizing the malice of mobbers to verdant forests signifying restoration, landscapes are at the heart of meaning-making in Christensen's paintings. Repeatedly, landscapes—and especially wildernesses or forests—work to tell the story just as much as the characters do. With his symbolic wildernesses, Christensen tapped into Christian iconography about exile and salvation, American ideas about expansion and progress, and Latter-day Saint beliefs about spiritual and material restoration.

Two of Christensen's earliest and most ambitious art projects—the Huntington Panorama and the Mormon Panorama—draw on these understandings of wilderness. They are especially good examples of how Christensen's landscapes fluctuate between the poles of exile and providence. For Christensen, wilderness is a cyclical concept beginning with a forested paradise, moving through periods of fallenness, and finally, through the labor of the righteous, becoming again a place where heaven and earth meet. His painted forests reflect Latter-day Saint ideas about originations and restorations as well as broader contemporary American movements and ideas.

The Huntington Panorama and the Mormon Panorama are long scrolls of consecutive images that were meant to be unrolled and viewed scene by scene. Panoramas were a popular artform in nineteenth-century England and the United States, both as a teaching tool and a type of entertainment. Panoramas often portrayed battle scenes, Bible stories, or dramatic moments from history. The earliest examples—in England in 1787 and in New York around 1819—were stationary large images, sometimes displayed in a full circle around the spectator. The first "moving panorama," in which a series of images on a long cloth scroll were unwound sequentially, appeared in London in 1829.[11] By the 1840s, moving panorama performances could be found throughout America. Presenters leaned into the greater degree of theatricality afforded by this format, adding immersive elements such as a live lecture, curtains, music, stage lighting, and even set design. Most panoramas attempted to create an uninterrupted view. For example, the popular moving panorama of the Mississippi River by John Bavard in the 1840s allowed audience members to imagine they were boating down the river as various scenes scrolled past. Around 1850, Montroville Wilson Dickeson and John Egan took a new approach, creating a panorama with twenty-five discrete scenes from the Mississippi Valley.[12] Christensen followed this method in both the Huntington and Mormon Panoramas.

For relatively isolated Latter-day Saint settlers in the Mountain West, panoramas were a window onto inaccessible places and cultures.[13] This was especially true in the 1870s—1890s for a rising generation born in Utah and raised without much contact with the outside world. Indeed, Christensen was not the first Latter-day Saint to employ the panorama format. In 1845, Church member Philo Dibble commissioned artists in Nauvoo to create a series of Church history scenes. These were enlarged to make a panorama that Dibble exhibited along with artifacts such as the death masks of Joseph and Hyrum Smith.[14] Another early Latter-day Saint panorama was made by Reuben Kirkham in 1883. It included twenty-three painted scenes (nonextant) of Book of Mormon stories.[15]

The first of Christensen's panoramas is now in the Church History Museum where it is called the *Untitled [Huntington/Lamanite Panorama]*. The Huntington Panorama was commissioned by Latter-day Saint missionary Dimick Huntington in the early 1870s to aid his missionary efforts with the Goshute, Ute, Paiute, and Shoshone.[16] The eleven scenes show:

Adam and Eve in the Garden,
Cain and Abel,
Noah and the Ark,
Lehi's Family Leaving Jerusalem,
Nephi Tied to the Mast,
Lehi's Family Arriving in the Promised Land,
Baptism of Jesus with the Holy Ghost in the Form of Dove,

Crucifixion of Christ,
Christ and His Disciples in the New World,
Moroni Hiding the Plates, and
Moroni Giving the Plates to Joseph Smith.

Shortly after completing that work, in 1878, Christensen began work on a larger project, called the Mormon Panorama, to recount events of early Mormon history. The twenty-three scenes (of which twenty-two are extant) were stitched together into a scroll. Christensen (and later his son Charles) used this panorama to teach Latter-day Saints in the Rocky Mountain region about the experiences of the earliest members who established the faith and moved west. The scenes are:

Joseph Smith's First Vision,
The Hill Cumorah,
Tarring and Feathering the Prophet,
Saints Driven from Jackson County Missouri,
Zion's Camp,
Mobbers on the Missouri River,
The Battle of Crooked River,
Haun's Mill,
The Arrest of Mormon Leaders,
Liberty Jail,
Leaving Missouri,
Joseph Preaching to the Indians,
Joseph Mustering the Nauvoo Legion,
Interior of Carthage Jail,
Exterior of Carthage Jail,
The Nauvoo Temple,
Burning of the Temple,
Crossing the Mississippi on the Ice,
The Battle of Nauvoo,
Catching Quails,
Winter Quarters,
Pioneers Crossing the Plains of Nebraska, and
Entering the Great Salt Lake Valley.

In both panoramas, Christensen's paintings display a dichotomy of the forest as both a foreboding place of trial and exile *and* a place of divine providence. The late nineteenth century was a time of change and upheaval for the Latter-day Saints. Members of the Church were negotiating a delicate relationship with the Indigenous peoples around them. At the same time, tensions with the United States government were reaching a boiling point. Anti-Mormon sentiment still ran high in America, and questions about polygamy and Utah statehood loomed large. Many members of the Church felt their liberties were threatened by the government. Although the Mormon Panorama covered history from half a century earlier, it was very much informed by the concerns of late-nineteenth-century Latter-day Saints about religious pluralism.[17] In the Huntington Panorama and Mormon Panorama, Christensen drew from Western traditions about the dual character of wilderness. In these monumental works, he created a religious and political commentary by using forests to outline physical and spiritual boundaries, mediate encounters with the divine, and privilege cultivation of the land.

Outlining Boundaries

In both the Huntington and Mormon panoramas, wilderness, usually represented by a forest, visualizes Latter-day Saint ideas about boundaries, injustice, sin, and banishment. Both sinners and saints find themselves at the threshold of the forest, though for different reasons. For instance, the Huntington Panorama begins with a scene of Adam and Eve ensconced in an idyllic forest. The second panel, though, turns the forest on its head as sin is introduced into the world. In *Cain and Abel* (Fig. 2.1), Cain flees from a sunlit open space and into the dark forest after murdering his brother. Art historian Laura Allred Hurtado points out the symbolism of the composition, saying, "The diagonal formed by the right side of the tree at the center of the painting separates an open, enlightened space from a dark, constricted one . . . Cain's hurried retreat into a closed, shadowed world suggests the spiritual costs of turning from God."[18] The forest is used here to demarcate a frontier—the line between good and evil, or civilization and savagery. In the image, Cain literally turns his back on the area of cleared ground, the altars of religion, and their accompanying emblems of agriculture (squash and a lamb), choosing instead a lawless existence in the forest. From the first image of Eden to this second image, the forest, through the fall of man, has changed from a site of innocent origin to a

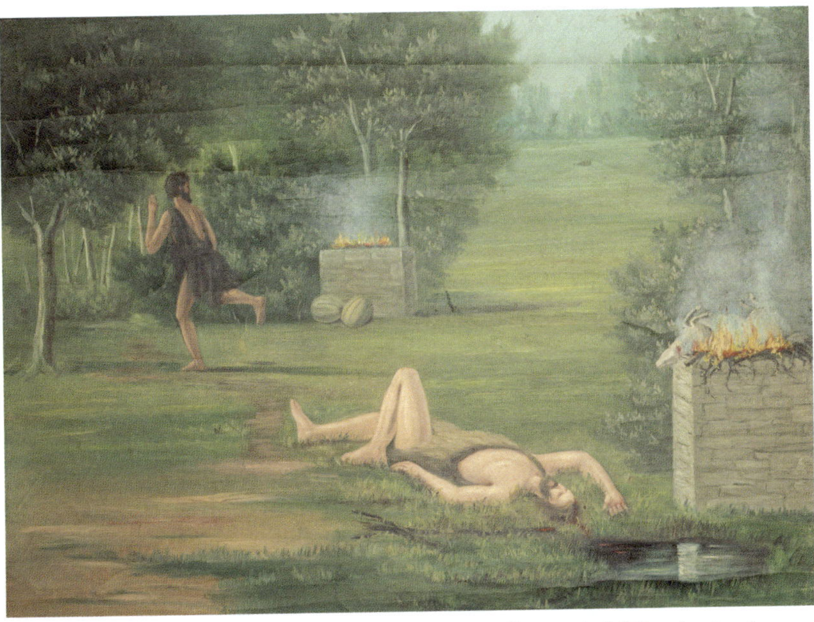

Figure 2.1 C. C. A. Christensen, "Cain and Abel," *Untitled [Huntington/ Lamanite Panorama]*, c. 1871–1875, oil on linen, 26 × 24 inches, Church History Museum, The Church of Jesus Christ of Latter-day Saints.

site of sin. The cleared, agricultural land with its altars, by contrast, is the site of religion.

The image aligns with historian Henry Nash Smith's argument that in nineteenth-century America, "the frontier of agricultural settlement was universally recognized as the line separating civilization from savagery."[19] Beginning with the earliest Puritan settlers, Americans viewed the advancing line of civilization against wilderness as a tangible testament to the triumph of good over evil. Man's ability to tame the wilderness and transform it into something productive was seen as a material witness to the power of Christian redemption.[20] Later, in the mid-nineteenth century, American pioneers tackling the frontier continued to see themselves, as scholar Roderick Frazier Nash puts it, "as agents in the regenerating process that turned the ungodly and useless into a beneficent civilization."[21]

This boundary created by wilderness, and its implications of exile and restoration, is a theme throughout the Huntington panorama. In the fourth

Huntington panel, *Lehi's Family Leaving Jerusalem* (Fig. 2.2), righteous people are forced into the wilderness. Citizens of Jerusalem threatened Lehi's life after he warned about the city's impending destruction. Instructed by God to leave the city in a dream (perhaps for immediate protection as well as escape from the coming Babylonian captivity), Lehi fled into the wilderness, which Christensen depicted as a refuge for the family. Lehi, Sariah, and their sons—Nephi, Sam, Laman, and Lemuel—are shown just outside the city walls as they move into the untamed desert wilderness. The people carry only a few small bundles. Nephi's bow and arrows and dagger indicate that the family will rely on the providential bounty of the wilderness to survive. The landscape helps relay the moral of the story, which is that they have chosen to follow God even though it means exile from man. The wilderness thus represents not just a physical separation from the city but also a spiritual one.

Tellingly, the same story (but with Latter-day Saint figures in nineteenth-century America) is told in the later Mormon Panorama: A righteous group

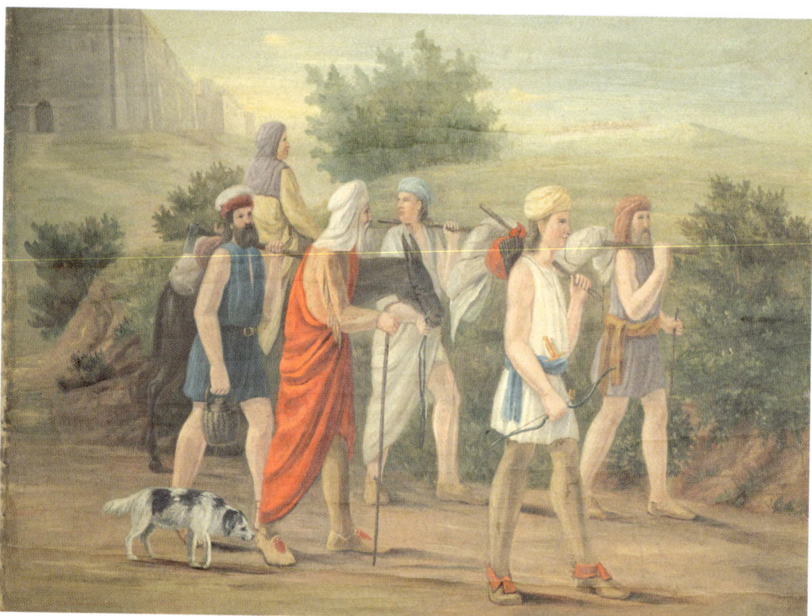

Figure 2.2 C. C. A. Christensen, "Lehi's Family Leaving Jerusalem," *Untitled [Huntington/Lamanite Panorama]*, c. 1871–1875, oil on linen, 26 × 24 inches, Church History Museum, The Church of Jesus Christ of Latter-day Saints.

of people is persecuted for their beliefs and forced to flee into the wilderness. They are then led to an unspoiled promised land where they work to clear the land and build Zion. But, in a striking contrast with the Huntington Panorama narrative, where the failure of ancient people to keep the covenant resulted in the loss of their civilization, the Mormon Panorama ends with the establishment of Zion.

In the Mormon Panorama, the wilderness marks the divide between right and wrong, civilization and wildness, and acceptance and exile. The entire Mormon Panorama can be read as a meditation on the nineteenth-century Latter-day Saint experience of being unjustly pushed out of society, finding sustenance and protection in the providential wilderness, and finally emerging on the other side of the forest to create a new and better society.[22] The Mormon Panorama opens with a portrayal of the young Joseph Smith seeing God the Father and His Son in a vision while in a grove near his family farm in Palmyra, New York.[23] The next scene shows the angel Moroni delivering ancient records to Joseph Smith within the forested Hill Cumorah in New York. Then, with only two or three exceptions, all the remaining scenes depict violence inflicted upon the Latter-day Saints and their ordeals in moving west to escape persecution. These ideas about persecution, chosen status, and restoration still permeate Latter-day Saint thought today, in part due to Christensen's emotionally engaging retelling that solidified this narrative in the minds of the people.

Repeatedly, in the Mormon Panorama, the forest plays a symbolic role that is integral to the narrative. Compare, for example, the third and fourth scenes of the Mormon Panorama: *Tarring and Feathering the Prophet* (Fig. 2.3) and *Saints Driven from Jackson County Missouri* (Fig. 2.4). Compositionally, the central action of both scenes takes place on the dividing line between forest on the left and orderly homes on the right. In this liminal space, chaos rules. In *Tarring and Feathering*, a group of men haul Joseph Smith away from civilization and into the dark woods. The men beat Smith with sticks and pull his shirt open in preparation for hot tar. The men intend to finish the job under cover of the forest. The two men in front—carrying a lantern, a sack of feathers, and a rail—lead the way into the woods. The bare branches of the winter trees claw at the sky, adding to the sense of violence. Although it looks as if the men have plenty of room there on a patch of cleared ground, they are moving into the forest. Why would it matter unless they knew their actions were beyond the bounds of acceptable

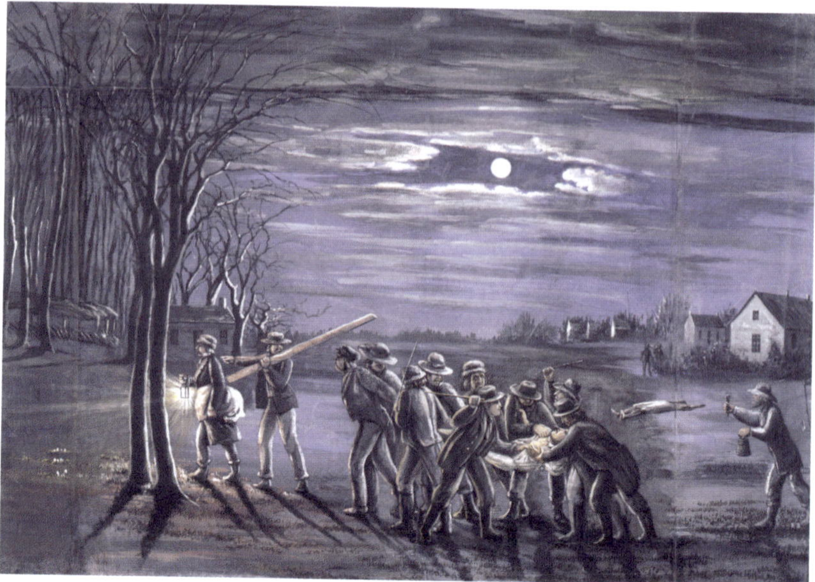

Figure 2.3 C. C. A. Christensen, *Tarring and Feathering the Prophet*, c. 1878, tempera on muslin, 78¼ × 114¼ inches. Brigham Young University Museum of Art, gift of the grandchildren of C. C. A. Christensen, 1970.

behavior? The forest somehow provides cover for the mob; the same rules do not apply once you cross that line.

We are presented with a similar composition in *Saints Driven from Jackson County Missouri*. Only now, the violence takes place in daylight and is directed not just at the leader of the group but at all its members. The movement is again from right to left, as the Saints are forced out of their homes and into the forest. In the central foreground, a mother carrying her infant is highlighted by her white blouse and yellow skirt. Close behind her, three darkly clad men brandishing rifles push her toward the forest. The visual emphasis on this group symbolizes the larger context of brutality against innocence. To the right, an older man fighting off a mobber is aided by his elderly wife, who grabs the mobber from behind. The man's discarded cane is on the ground, as is the woman's spilled pail of milk. To the left, a young wife pleads for the life of her injured husband. In the background, a mother and two children stand frozen in no-man's land and look directly out at the viewer. The group is silhouetted against a burning

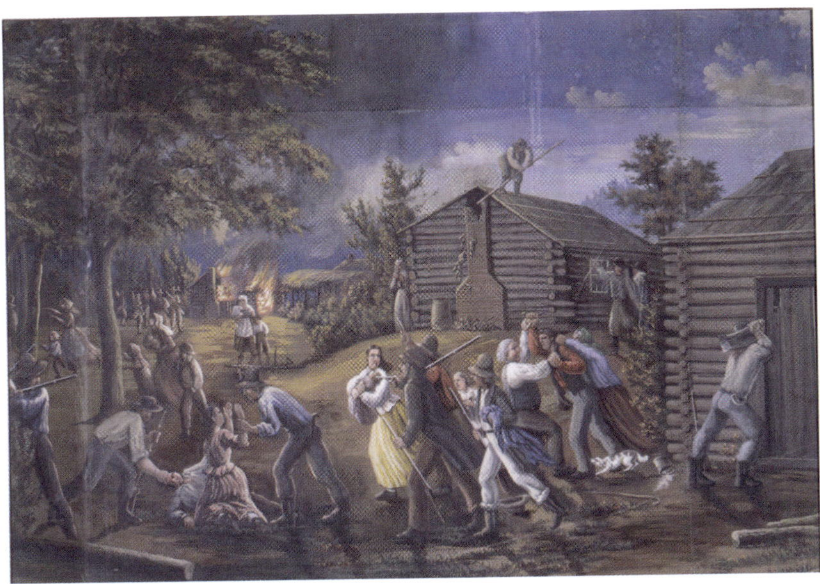

Figure 2.4 C. C. A. Christensen, *Saints Driven from Jackson County Missouri*, c. 1878, tempera on muslin, 77¼ × 113 inches. Brigham Young University Museum of Art, gift of the grandchildren of C. C. A. Christensen, 1970.

home in a grotesque parody of the picture of domestic bliss. Taken together, these vignettes show a world gone topsy-turvy. It is the innocent Saints who must flee into the protective forest, and it is the armed mobbers who take over civilized space.

The forest can be a cover for evil or a refuge for goodness, but it always marks a boundary. People who exist within a forest, whether by choice or by force, are understood to live outside the normal rules. Christensen powerfully tapped into long-standing concepts about forest and wilderness in his art. In the Mormon Panorama, movement from civilization to the forest/wilderness is always shown as a movement from right to left. Christensen may draw on long-standing Christian and European heraldic concepts about the left side, which associate it with evil.[24] The direction of movement switches, however, in the very last scene, *Entering the Great Salt Lake Valley* (Fig. 2.5). Here, the wagon train of Latter-day Saint refugees emerges from the forest on the left to move into the wide-open valley on the right. The implication is that, having made it through the ordeals of the

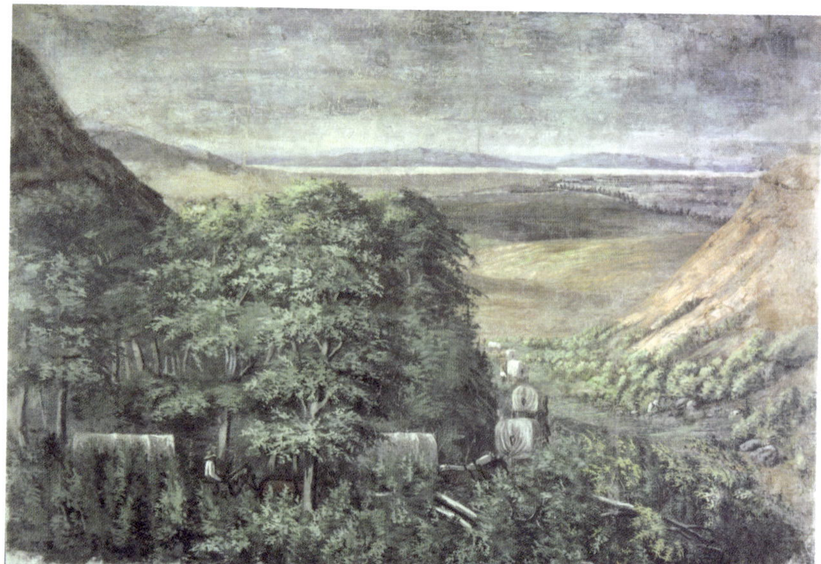

Figure 2.5 C. C. A. Christensen, *Entering the Great Salt Lake Valley*, c. 1878, tempera on muslin, 77¼ × 113 inches. Brigham Young University Museum of Art, gift of the grandchildren of C. C. A. Christensen, 1970.

forest, the Saints are free to establish a more just and righteous civilization than the one out of which they were forced. In both nineteenth-century Latter-day Saint thought and in this painting, the forest/wilderness was seen as a very real boundary—both physical and spiritual—between the Saints and the United States.

Mediating the Divine

Despite long-standing temporal and spiritual fears of wilderness, the Euro-American Christian tradition also looks to the forest as a site of divine encounter or as a link to a more perfect or holy time. If the *selva antica* is where man first knew God, perhaps the forest is where man can find God again. In this tradition, nineteenth-century American Protestant revivalist groups saw the forest as a place to commune with the divine.[25] As historian Brett Grainger explains, the forest setting allowed nineteenth-century American Christians to imagine a shared site with God's anciently chosen people:

> In field preaching, camp meetings, and outdoor baptism, countless men and women sought salvation in the open . . . But nature's theater was more than a scenic backdrop. By layering fields, forests, and streams with allusions to biblical sites and by erecting memorials to supernatural events, antebellum evangelicals constructed spiritual landscapes that enhanced their distinctive quest for 'vital piety,' a felt sense of abundant presence in the here and now.[26]

The forest conjures ideas of a simpler time, when the presence of deity dwelt closer to man. Returning to the forest was a way of seeking to restore that relationship between God and man. In the forest, worshippers could separate themselves from city life and demonstrate their independence from more established churches. Traveling Baptist and Methodist preachers often held outdoor meetings and taught from atop a rock.

Christensen effectively employed the *selva antica* in the first scene of the Huntington Panorama, *Adam and Eve in the Garden* (Fig. 2.6). The figures are enveloped within and even covered up by nature, as if they are united

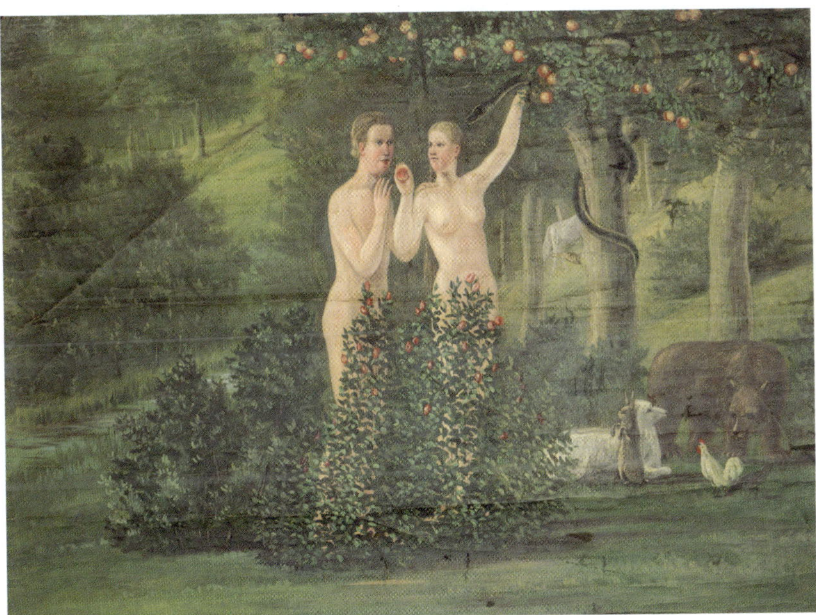

Figure 2.6 C. C. A. Christensen, "Adam and Eve in the Garden," *Untitled [Huntington/Lamanite Panorama]*, c. 1871–1875, oil on linen, 26 × 24 inches, Church History Museum, The Church of Jesus Christ of Latter-day Saints.

with it. The image closely resembles the most famous rendering of Adam and Eve: the legendary 1504 engraving by German artist Albrecht Dürer.[27] Trained at the Royal Danish Academy of Fine Arts in Copenhagen, Christensen would certainly have seen prints of Dürer's masterpiece. In both images, the scene takes place in a lush forest, with central human figures next to a serpent coiled around a tree. In both, the couple is surrounded by peaceful animals (Christensen charmingly adds a rooster and hen, staples of Utah settlement life). But there are also revealing differences between the two images. Whereas Dürer highlighted the human form—looking to classical Greek sculpture, live models, and his own theories of perfect human proportion—Christensen covers the lower halves of the bodies with foliage. Adam's angled position, with arm raised in front of him, closes off his figure even more. His awkward position emphasizes Eve's more open and graceful posture. Moreover, Dürer's monumental figures are highlighted just in front of the tree line, with only the suggestion of a forest behind them. But Christensen's couple is swallowed up in an expansive view of the forest that includes a hillside cutting across the picture plane to a stream at the lower left, varieties of trees and bushes, and flowers. In Christensen's vision, man does not stand apart from nature but rather is integrated with it. In the *selva antica*, man is united with God.

The presence of deity in the forest is visualized even more explicitly in other Huntington panels. *Christ and His Disciples in the New World* (Fig. 2.7) shows the resurrected Savior preaching to his chosen twelve Nephite disciples in the wilderness of ancient America. The figure of Christ is emphasized by its central placement, white robes, and diagonally outstretched arms. He speaks from atop a rock while the disciples sit or stand in various poses as they listen. The large buildings of the city sit under an open sky in the background, contrasting with the group of righteous men enclosed within the edges of a forest that fills the right third of the canvas. In this liminal space, Christ calls his disciples in ancient America to the work. Is the cityscape meant to represent an ancient American city? Perhaps the Egyptian-style pyramid and palm trees are Christensen's simplistic shorthand for any ancient culture on any continent. But if so, how do we explain the contrast of tall palm trees with the leafy deciduous trees in which Christ and his apostles are ensconced? Perhaps the hazy pyramid and palm trees are a vision of the Old World. Perhaps they illustrate that Jesus is telling his New World disciples about his ministry in the ancient Near East.

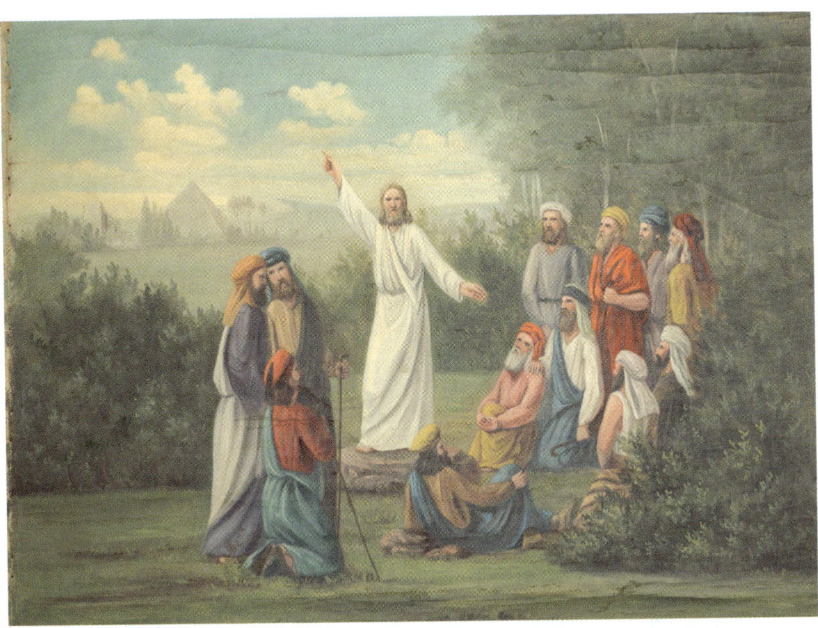

Figure 2.7 C. C. A. Christensen, "Christ and His Disciples in the New World," *Untitled [Huntington/Lamanite Panorama]*, c. 1871–1875, oil on linen, 26 × 24 inches, Church History Museum, The Church of Jesus Christ of Latter-day Saints.

In any event, the exposed city is quite clearly presented in contradistinction to the rustic simplicity of the forest. Even as a boy in 1820, Joseph Smith apparently understood the forest as a locus for divine connection. He wrote that his vision of God the Father and Jesus Christ occurred after he "retired to the woods" to "ask of God."[28] The writings of Smith and others indicate that the woods continued to hold a special spiritual significance for many nineteenth-century members of the Church. For instance, in 1835, William McLellin wrote that with a few other men, "This day we spent from 9 till 3. together in the woods in prayrs [*sic*] and contemplation endeavouring [*sic*] to obtain an open vision but we did not although. we felt that we drew very near to God."[29] Later, one of those men, Orson Hyde, writing in 1840 as a member of the Quorum of the Twelve Apostles, recorded that he "preached this day to a large audience in the woods" while in New Jersey.[30] This view of the forest as a place to connect with God and to throw off the evils and excesses of society characterized thinking in the broader contemporary American society too.

Christensen's image of Christ preaching on the edges of a forest nicely parallels nineteenth-century Protestant images that showed ministers speaking in nature. Such compositions were common up through the antebellum period. In both the Protestant images and the Christensen painting, the artists were visualizing a theology and religious practice that looked to nature to mediate the divine. Moving outside the bounds of the city allowed believers to return to something more hidden, interior, primitive, and sacred. In that sense, perhaps the forest also symbolized a longing for the promised paradise to come.

The final panel of the Huntington Panorama brings things full circle by showing the forest redeemed through the restoration in *Moroni Giving the Plates to Joseph Smith* (Fig. 2.8). It follows a panel depicting Moroni and Mormon hiding the record of their people in a hillside (Fig. 2.9). The sparse

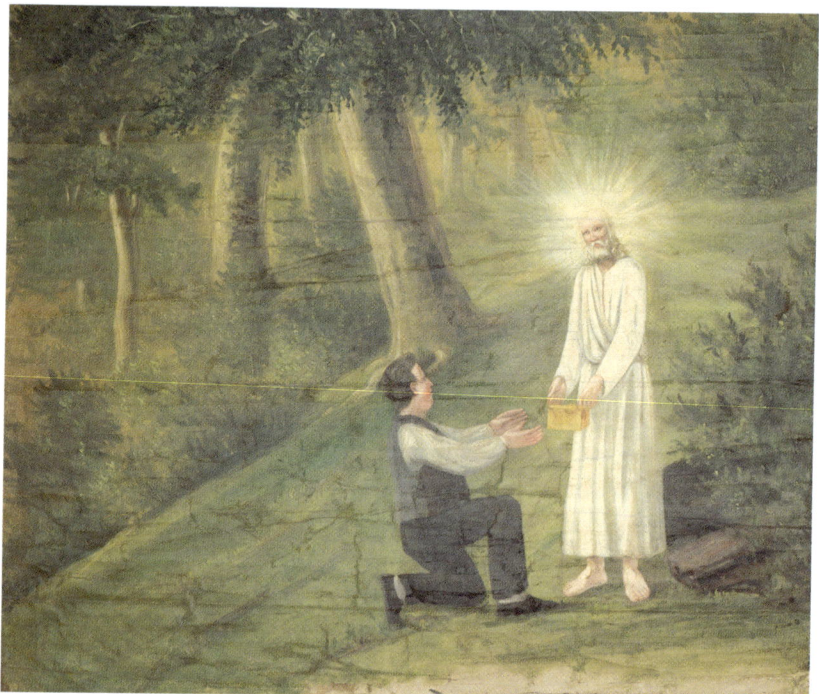

Figure 2.8 C. C. A. Christensen, "Moroni Giving the Plates to Joseph Smith," *Untitled [Huntington/Lamanite Panorama]*, c. 1871–1875, oil on linen, 26 × 24 inches, Church History Museum, The Church of Jesus Christ of Latter-day Saints.

vegetation on the hill of the Moroni/Mormon panel explodes into a dense forest in this final latter-day scene. Christensen makes it clear that this is the same topographical site, with the same steep hill, rocks, and bushes marking the spot where the plates were buried anciently in the previous panel. He indicates the passage of centuries by moving from short, thin tree trunks to tall, thick ones. The dramatic hill diagonally bisecting the canvas in both panels intentionally echoes the one seen in the first Garden of Eden scene. The forest is imagined as returning to its original state, as Moroni and Joseph Smith usher in the restoration of God's promises. The land is redeemed, and by extension, so are Lehi's descendants, who Christensen and Huntington believed to be the Indigenous populations to whom they showed these images.

By visually linking the Hill Cumorah to the site of ancient American prophets from the Book of Mormon, as well as to the biblical Garden of Eden, Christensen attaches strong meaning to a specific location. Seeking this type of connection between the landscape and biblical events was a

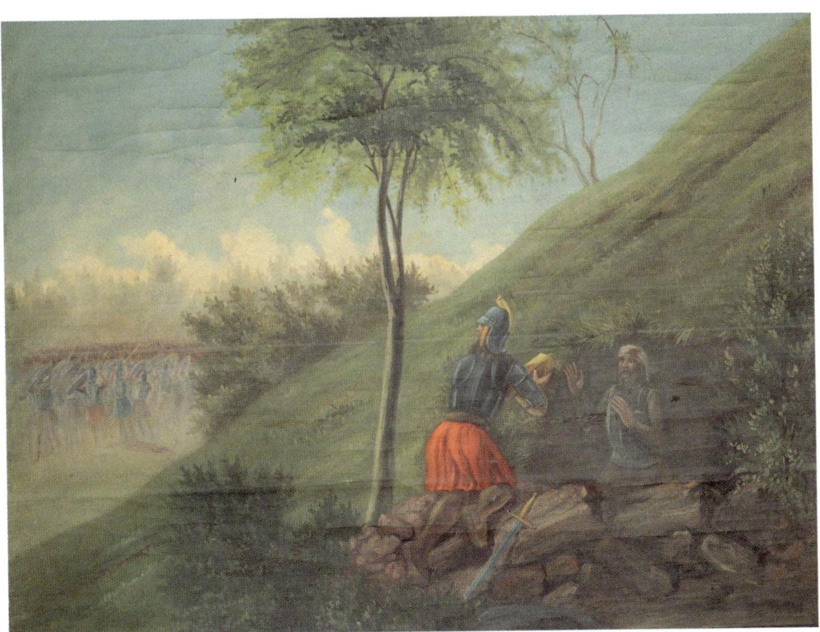

Figure 2.9 C. C. A. Christensen, "Moroni Hiding the Plates," *Untitled [Huntington/Lamanite Panorama]*, c. 1871–1875, oil on linen, 26 × 24 inches, Church History Museum, The Church of Jesus Christ of Latter-day Saints.

common practice among American evangelicals in the nineteenth century. In looking back to the harmony between man and nature found in the Garden of Eden, they were also looking forward to a promise of that kind of harmony in the millennium.[31] The practice of connecting contemporary geographical sites with scriptural events and figures was also common among nineteenth-century Latter-day Saints in Utah. As historian Christopher Blythe explains, "this sacralizing lens transformed unfamiliar mountain ranges" and "inscribed the narrative of the Book of Mormon onto the mountain and desert landscape of Deseret."[32] Although by the 1870s Church members were gathered in the Great Basin, far from the Hill Cumorah in New York, Christensen's painting memorializes that sacred place where man, the divine, and nature powerfully met. Underlining the importance of this scene, Christensen later repainted it as the second panel of his Mormon Panorama—the only scene to appear in both projects.

Similarly, the Mormon Panorama indicates the presence of deity, or at least of divine providence, in the forest. And it explicitly draws on biblical models of exodus and preservation to do so. In *Crossing the Mississippi on the Ice* (Fig. 2.10), streams of refugees flow out of the large city

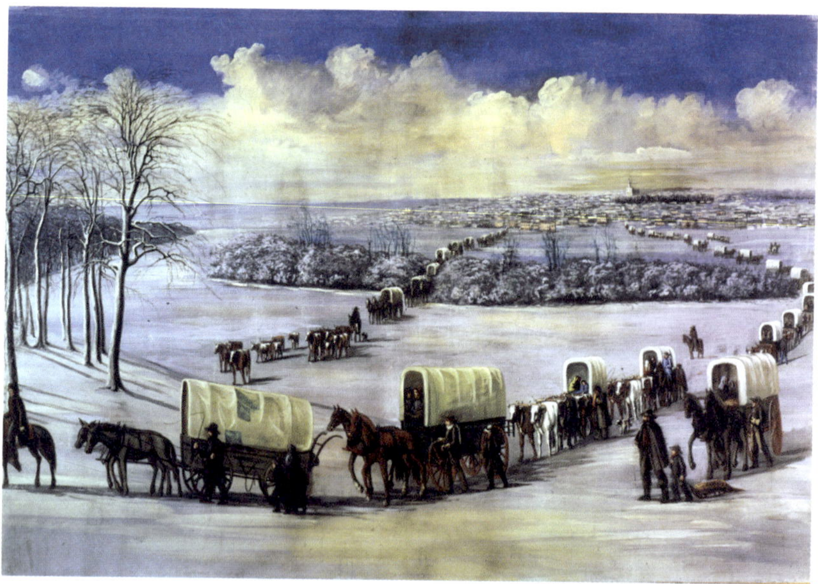

Figure 2.10 C. C. A. Christensen, *Crossing the Mississippi on the Ice*, c. 1878, tempera on muslin, 77⅞ × 114 inches. Brigham Young University Museum of Art, gift of the grandchildren of C. C. A. Christensen, 1970.

of Nauvoo, Illinois, and into the wilderness. Pressured by mob persecution and demands by the governor of Illinois, the Latter-day Saints were finally compelled to leave the state in the winter of 1846. In the painting, the dramatic curving lines of two wagon trains pull the viewer's eye back toward the distant city with its prominent temple. The vast swath of frozen, snow-covered river adds to the bleak mood. Christensen highlights several parallels with the exodus of the ancient Hebrews from Egypt. First, there are indications that the party fled quickly: The beasts of burden are whatever the people had on hand—a mix of oxen, horses, and mules—and the foremost covered wagon has prominent, hastily patched repairs to its canvas. Second, the freezing of the mighty Mississippi River is presented as a miracle equivalent to the parting of the Red Sea. In his accompanying lecture for this image, Christensen explained, "This Bridge of ice was made by a kind Providence at the time when the lives of our saints were at stake."[33]

Allusions to the biblical exodus are also conspicuous in *Catching Quails* (Fig. 2.11). Here, we see the miraculous appearance of flocks of quail within the rudimentary woodland camp of the Saints outside Nauvoo. These were

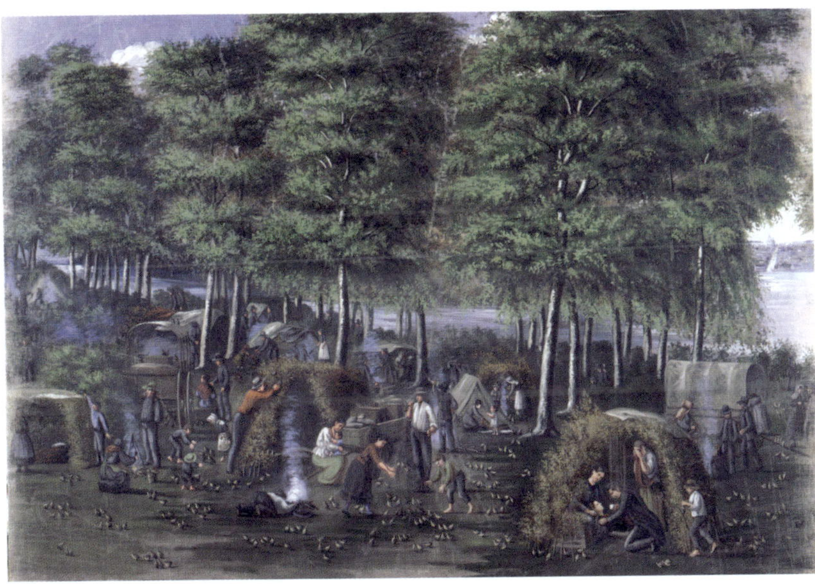

Figure 2.11 C. C. A. Christensen, *Catching Quails*, c. 1878, tempera on muslin, 76¼ × 113 inches. Brigham Young University Museum of Art, gift of the grandchildren of C. C. A. Christensen, 1970.

the final refugees from the city—the 700 or so who were too old, sick, infirm, or poor to make the journey the prior winter. In September, these remaining Latter-day Saints were attacked and forced out of Nauvoo. In their forest encampment, the appearance of quail for food was seen as a reenactment of the blessing of quails and manna received by the ancient Israelites.[34] As in the biblical exodus of God's chosen people, the Latter-day Saints saw themselves provided with protection and food in the wilderness. Christensen's painting is dominated by the large trees of the forest—the human figures and quail are comparatively small. The imposing forest contrasts with the distant view of Nauvoo across the river. Symbolically, then, the forest points to the exile of these people from civilization but also references their protection by God. Christensen spelled this out quite clearly in his panorama lecture:

> Here they are at a point of starvation, but true to God and his cause. They humbly asked God to come to their rescue in this hour of trouble, starvation staring them in the face. The Lord caused these birds to come by the meriods [*sic*] swarming on the camp grounds and in the tents and were so tame that men, women and children could catch them with their hands as you see them doing. Thus you see how the Lord hears and answers the prayers of those who come to him in humility and faith.[35]

Similarly, within the text of the Book of Mormon, the forest is sometimes presented as a source of the food that made possible the nomadic life of the Lehite pilgrims. The whole of 1 Nephi 16 considers the wilderness as a place where God provides food for the righteous, and yet also a place where everyone inevitably suffers. The narrative fluctuates between the people finding wild game and rejoicing, and then enduring privations, fatigue, and sorrow. Even while still wandering in the arid wilderness outside Jerusalem, Lehi's family hunted animals: "We did take our bows and our arrows, and go forth into the wilderness to slay food for our families."[36] There are indications that God directed the hunting, according to the people's faith, through the Liahona: "We did follow the directions of the ball, which led us in the more fertile parts of the wilderness."[37] Nephi even says that God enabled them to eat raw meat and told them, "I will make thy food become sweet, that ye cook it not."[38] Once in the new world, Nephi recounts that "we did find upon the land of promise, as we journeyed in the wilderness, that there were beasts in the forests of every kind, both the cow and the ox, and the ass and the horse, and the goat and the wild goat, and all manner of wild animals, which were for the use of men."[39] Christensen's *Catching Quails* scene draws on these Latter-day Saint beliefs in the divine providence of food in the forest.

Wilderness, often understood in the European and American traditions as forest, can represent a primitive place to find God and to be protected by God. The concept of wilderness permeates the Old and New Testaments. Even Eden is frequently visualized in Western art and literature as not so much a garden as a forest. The Book of Mormon also takes up the theme of human experience with the wilderness or forest. And early Latter-day Saint leaders, including Joseph Smith, understood the forest as a geographical place where contact with divinity was more likely. Christensen's panoramas similarly visualize forests as places that may involve ordeal but where God can reveal himself to his chosen people.

Cultivating Zion

Forests mark boundaries and allow for spiritual connection, and in American Latter-day Saint thought, they also served as the raw material for building God's kingdom on earth. In his art, Christensen waffles between praising the clearing of forest to make way for agriculture and enlightenment and harboring a longing for untouched sylvan land that represents divine providence. It was a dichotomy that not just the Latter-day Saints but all of America was grappling with at the time, as frontier expansion reached its limits in the late nineteenth century. In 1891, the federal Forest Reserve Act was passed in an attempt to manage and preserve the dwindling great American forest. Perhaps Christensen's loving treatment of woodland in his art was partly motivated by a longing for an earlier time or concerns about the changes he saw happening in the landscape.

The idea of wilderness as the place for restoration and for building a righteous community was common in American thought. For centuries, European Protestants had latched onto the metaphor of braving the symbolic wilderness to seek God, and of transforming the wilderness to build Zion and thus spread purely distilled eternal truths. In America, though, the wilderness was a literal presence. According to English professor Gustav Blanke, the forest became an even more potent symbol for the Latter-day Saints as a subset of nineteenth-century Americans. Their own lived experience in the actual American wilderness "perfectly supported the Mormons' view of themselves as a people especially chosen to be tried, a people set apart for a holy struggle that would establish their divine merit in the eyes of the world."[40]

The Huntington Panorama promotes the view that the forest must be cultivated—and ultimately redeemed—to become promised land. In *Lehi's Family Arriving in the Promised Land* (Fig. 2.12), the emphasis is as much on a massive leafy tree as it is on Nephi. The prophet kneels under the tree and raises his arms in a gesture of prayer and thanksgiving. The land appears uninhabited but desirable. The rest of the family is still making their way out of the boat, and the line of their movement pulls the viewer's eye from Nephi back into the edges of forest and then out to the shore. The family, then, is shown moving from under an open sky and into the dense canopy of an untouched, Eden-like forest. Nephi's posture is echoed a few panels later in the figure of Joseph Smith as he receives the plates from the angel Moroni. Both Nephi and Smith are depicted kneeling next to a large tree

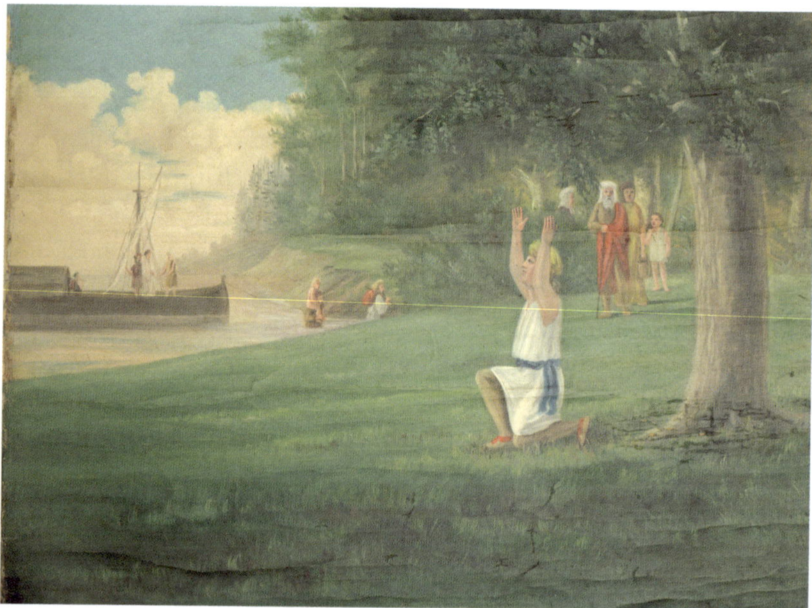

Figure 2.12 C. C. A. Christensen, "Lehi's Family Arriving in the Promised Land," *Untitled [Huntington/Lamanite Panorama]*, c. 1871–1875, oil on linen, 26 × 24 inches, Church History Museum, The Church of Jesus Christ of Latter-day Saints.

while communicating with the divine. The prophetic calling of both men is visually tied here to restoration of the land. Both men work to create a geographical space for God's chosen people. In both cases, this work is understood to involve building a new civilization—one modeled on the old one but perfected by a closer union with the divine and thus attaining even greater heights.

For those familiar with the Book of Mormon narrative, this scene of arrival in the promised land carries a sense that the dense virgin forest must be changed and cleared to make way for the teeming cities of Lehi's future descendants. Repeatedly, the Book of Mormon itself privileges agriculture and human order imposed on wilderness. Indeed, the most famous symbol from the Book of Mormon is a lone, carefully cultivated fruit tree beside a river and handrail.[41] Jacob's allegory of the olive orchard also heavily emphasizes the importance of God-directed human work in domesticating and maintaining the flora.[42] The book of Helaman, written about 500 years after Lehi's arrival, describes parts of the land as "rendered desolate and without timber, because of the many inhabitants who had before inherited the land."[43] Elsewhere, in the book of Enos, the agricultural habits of the righteous Nephites who "till the land, and raise all manner of grain, and of fruit, and flocks of herds" are contrasted with the fallen Lamanites who are "wild, and ferocious, and a blood-thirsty people, full of idolatry and filthiness; feeding upon beasts of prey; dwelling in tents, and wandering about in the wilderness."[44] In these passages, Latter-day Saint scripture lauds agricultural order and describes forests not as appropriate places to live but as God-given raw material useful for building civilizations.

This view dovetails with nineteenth-century American ideas about taming the wilderness to advance and expand civilization. American identity was largely bound up with a vision of vast fields of grain springing up before an ever-receding wilderness frontier. The industrious and independent American farmer, clearing the forest to make way for agriculture and civilization, anchored this vision.[45] The idyllic vision of the pastoral or rural did not mean untamed wilderness but rather a well-ordered and cultivated land.[46] American dreams of Manifest Destiny were bound up with the duty of God-fearing people to reclaim the land from chaos, wilderness, and savagery, and to turn it into a fruitful paradise.

A visualization of the land returning to a garden-like, paradisiacal state also permeated statements by nineteenth-century Church leaders. Many leaders spoke about the role of the Church in redeeming American land. For instance, in 1832, William W. Phelps said that as Church members worked to improve their lands in Jackson County, Missouri, the land would "become like Eden or the garden of the Lord."[47] Later, Brigham Young said, "The Saints would take the 'fallen' deserts of northern Mexico . . . and turn them into the Garden of Eden."[48] Undergirding these statements is the belief that redemption of the land would happen not through the land returning to its natural state, but rather through the hard work of the people in clearing, cultivating, and transforming the land through agriculture. In a similar vein, Matthew Godfrey has described the way nineteenth-century Church members "believed that land was owned by God, that wilderness needed to be improved to redeem it from its fallen state, that God used nature and the earth to both reward and punish the righteous, and that the physical possession of tracts of land demonstrated God's approval of them as a people."[49] Nineteenth-century Latter-day Saints understood their role in cultivating and redeeming the land as parallel to the way the ancient Nephites did similar work. Taken together, Christensen's Huntington Panorama and Mormon Panorama tell this story of how, across time, God's chosen people are always called to tame wilderness to build Zion.

For Latter-day Saints, building the city of God is not something only done anciently, nor simply a promise for the future. It is the work of the Saints right now. Accordingly, in the Mormon Panorama, the transformative drama is made contemporary. The *Winter Quarters* (Fig. 2.13) panel depicts a settlement constructed by the Latter-day Saints in December 1846. Evicted at gunpoint from Nauvoo, the Saints crossed the frozen Mississippi River but were not able to continue to the Rocky Mountains until spring. They set up a make-shift encampment near Omaha to wait out the winter weather. Compositionally, Christensen's painting brings attention to the landscape. This is more than just a scene of pioneers moving westward—it is a scene of a chosen people caught in a liminal geographical space. With the dangerous river to their east (separating them from the United States government and from extra-legal persecutors) and the untamed frontier to their west, the Latter-day Saints must carve a new path into the wilderness. Already, Christensen hints at the order this group will impose on the American forest. The sweeping view of tidy log cabins is a kind of man-made forest. These pioneers are harnessing the possibilities of the forest to build Zion. With the river now thawed under blue skies, we

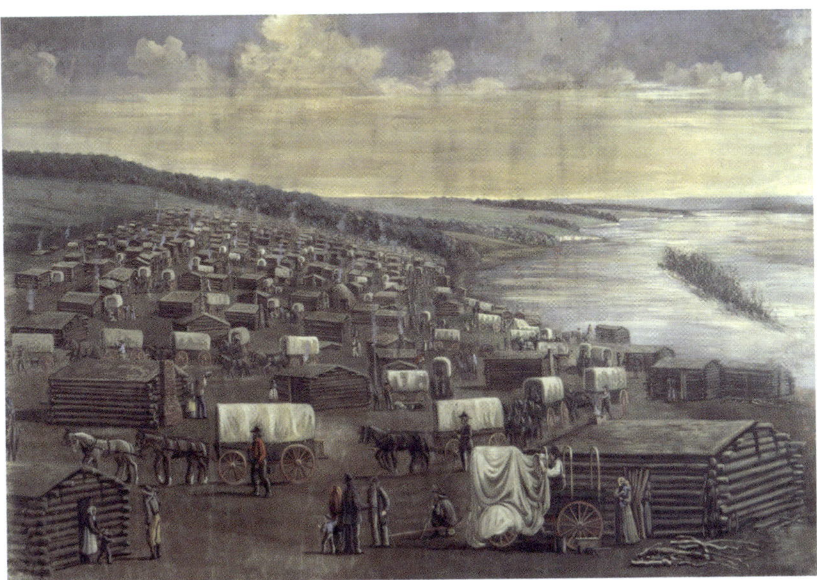

Figure 2.13 C. C. A. Christensen, *Winter Quarters*, c. 1878, tempera on muslin, 76¾ × 113¾ inches. Brigham Young University Museum of Art, gift of the grandchildren of C. C. A. Christensen, 1970.

see wagon trains starting westward from the camp, bringing civilization with them.

In the late nineteenth century, as American wilderness was conquered and the westward surge ebbed, the value of the forest for purposes other than strict utilitarianism came into focus.[50] Latter-day Saints and other Americans saw value in the aesthetic functions of the primitive forest and the role it could play in promoting national identity. They also began to express concerns about long-term stewardship of resources. Even the Book of Mormon implies that timber resources must be protected from overuse. In Helaman, after large-scale destruction of the forest for cities and homes, the people implemented a new plan to "suffer whatsoever tree should spring up upon the face of the land that it should grow up, that in time they might have timber to build."[51] As a Utah settler, Christensen himself gained experience farming and tending the land. In his later years, he wrote many editorials about the proper distribution and use of water rights in the Utah settlements. Like so many European and American exceptionalists before him, Christensen believed that material progress, largely symbolized by the cultivation of wilderness into productive sites of agriculture and civilization, was the destiny and duty of God's chosen people.

Conclusions

Drawing on the dual role of wilderness in Western thought, Christensen painted landscapes to help tell a story. Forests are a powerful symbol because they can represent both sides of the same coin—either a place of evil and deprivation or the site of spiritual encounter and abundance. Moreover, *how* the forest is used is a critical component of Christensen's artwork. Themes of land occupation run throughout his oeuvre, and especially in his various panorama series. Much of his subject matter revolves around the Mormon migration west and the movement of Lehi's family from Jerusalem to the Americas, both of which encompass ideas about wilderness, promised land, and restoration. From their own experience of traversing the American wilderness in the mid-nineteenth century, the Latter-day Saints saw the forest as a symbol for their physical and spiritual separation from the world, their experience of divine encounter and deliverance, and their God-given ability to impose order and facilitate the redemption of the land.

Christensen painted his most iconic and widely viewed images in the 1870s through the 1890s. At that time, several converging factors—renewed pressure from the federal government over polygamy and Utah statehood, rising tensions with local native populations, and concerns about environmental changes due to deforestation and overgrazing—kept issues of land ownership and use a central issue for Latter-day Saints. At this pivotal moment, as the Saints drew on lessons from their past to navigate new challenges at the end of the nineteenth century, Christensen concretized Latter-day Saint thought in both his art and writing. Considering the significance of the Mormon Panorama, Steven Harper suggested that "Christensen's depiction of past persecutions would have resonated with Latter-day Saints who were dealing with a hostile government and Protestant establishment. The illustrated narration catalyzed memory recursion."[52] Christensen helped shape Latter-day Saint memory, thought, and self-identity at the close of the nineteenth century.

Christensen's emblematic use of forests in his history paintings largely parallels beliefs from other American revivalist groups about how divinity is found (or lost) in nature and about the role of covenant people in redeeming the land, but with a distinctly Mormon bent. In Christensen's paintings, as much as cultivation is praised, it is always in the forest that man meets God. Forests become symbols of God's promises to his chosen people, and the restoration of the forest is equated with the restoration of the Gospel through Joseph Smith and the accompanying redemption of the people.

CHAPTER THREE

Old World Style and New World Scripture

The Book of Mormon Paintings

As one of the first artists to visualize Restoration scripture, experience, and doctrine, C. C. A. Christensen broke fresh ground in his religious art. He combined traditional European iconography with innovative and conspicuous Latter-day Saint symbolism. Although he is typically considered an American folk artist, Christensen's art has much in common with the Old World's legacy of academic history painting, Danish Golden Age art's emphasis on narrative and naturalism, and French Orientalism's preoccupation with historical detail and accuracy. Exemplary of this approach, Christensen's 1890 Book of Mormon painting series brings tropes of these European styles to bear on new scripture in a new world. Resituating Christensen's Book of Mormon paintings within the context of European art reveals insights into Latter-day Saint understandings of the function of religious artworks as narrative-driven, factually accurate witnesses to history and scripture.

At the Royal Danish Academy of Fine Arts, Christensen was taught a neoclassical academic style heavily influenced by a wave of Danish romantic nationalism. This movement encouraged subjects and styles that reflected their folk heritage. Even after he immigrated to Utah, Christensen's journals record that he studied European (and especially Danish) art on his Scandinavian missions in the 1860s and 1880s. Christensen, steeped in art memorializing the common man, was among the first to visualize Restoration theology, with its emphasis on materiality, accessibility, and historicity.

Even though Christensen's artworks are not well known today, the approach they embody had a lasting effect on the Latter-day Saint conception of the role of religious art. Moreover, through his Book of Mormon paintings and his writing, Christensen codified developing Latter-day Saint ideas about the nature of the divine. He developed a visual vocabulary that both reflected and encouraged early Latter-day Saints' concern with issues of divine embodiment and with defining humanity's relation to the divine. As Latter-day Saints wrestled with questions about the function of images in worship and with the embodied nature of divine beings, Christensen's art helped shape approaches to these topics.

Christensen's 1890 Book of Mormon Series

Although members of The Church of Jesus Christ of Latter-day Saints today enjoy thousands of images based on the Book of Mormon, nineteenth-century Saints had far fewer opportunities to engage with this type of art. In the nineteenth century, artists rarely attempted to illustrate scenes from the book. When they did, artists created the images for specific uses that did not result in wide viewership.[1] Leaders within the Church did not make a public appeal for Book of Mormon art until March of 1890, a full sixty years after the Book of Mormon was printed. At that time, George Q. Cannon, president of the Deseret Sunday School Union, led the call for a series of paintings illustrating the life of Nephi. The request asked for the following twelve scenes:

> Lehi preaching to the Jews,
> The departure of Lehi and his family from Jerusalem,
> The death of Laban,
> Lehi's vision of the iron rod,
> Nephi's vision of the virgin and child,
> The finding of the compass [Liahona],
> The building of the ship,
> The first sacrifice on the Promised Land,
> Lehi blessing his posterity,
> The separation of the Nephites and Lamanites,
> The building of the temple, and
> Nephi making the plates for the records.[2]

Ultimately, the Deseret Sunday School Union chose twelve scenes—ten by Christensen and two by George Ottinger. The final scenes deviate slightly from the original call for art, as there is no "death of Laban" or "Lehi's vision of the iron rod," but added are a depiction of Nephi retrieving the brass plates from Jerusalem and a scene of a daughter of Ishmael and her mother protecting Nephi from his brothers.

For decades, these twelve scenes were the most broadly disseminated and viewed images from the Book of Mormon. The Deseret Sunday School Union had the paintings made into colored lithographs and distributed these reproductions to Sunday School teachers.[3] The images were also serialized as grayscale lithographs in issues of the *Juvenile Instructor* from April 15 to October 1, 1891, alongside lessons written by George Reynolds to educate the youth of the Church. Christensen also exhibited his paintings inside Ephraim's Tabernacle in July 1890 and at the county fair in October 1890, where they received attention in the local newspaper.[4]

These early landmark Book of Mormon paintings are not well known today. It may be that their distinctive combination of Old-World academic history painting and folksy early American naivete felt out of step when the Church Correlation Department began to heavily use images in their materials in the 1960s and 1970s. Other artists and illustrators around that time—including Arnold Friberg, Robert Barrett, Tom Lovell, and Jerry Thompson—produced the Book of Mormon images that became iconic in Latter-day Saint culture. But Christensen's series was widely viewed by Church members for half a century and influenced how they thought about scripture. Even in the twentieth century, the 1915 silent film *The Life of Nephi*, produced by William A. Morton, clearly looked to Christensen's paintings for inspiration. In some instances, the film staging even directly copied the Christensen compositions.[5] Christensen's images of Nephi also showed up in editions of Reynolds's *The Story of the Book of Mormon*. For a generation or more, Church members used these Book of Mormon images to visualize the scriptures. Their importance in delineating Latter-day Saint iconography and belief is only beginning to be understood.

The original paintings are currently in the collection of the Church History Museum and are sometimes displayed at the Grandin Building of the Palmyra, New York historical site. But they are rarely used in the Church's manuals and materials and are generally unfamiliar to members of the Church today. This series has received even less scholarly attention than Christensen's scenes of early Church history. Yet, as some of the earliest, most widely viewed Book of Mormon artworks, these paintings merit more attention. The images influenced Latter-day Saint thought about the Book of Mormon and the nature of God, and they paved the way for a certain understanding about the narrative and moralizing function of religious art that still holds true.

Traditional Tropes: Art as a Witness to History

Long before painting his Book of Mormon series, Christensen had already demonstrated his belief in the power of images to witness and record historical events. Two decades earlier, in the 1870s, Christensen painted the Mormon Panorama, a series of twenty-three large scenes of early Church history. He traveled throughout Western Church settlements, showing that panorama and expounding on it with a prepared lecture. In the paintings and the lecture, Christensen included details gleaned from photographs, drawings, and written accounts to make the presentation feel historically accurate.[6] He wanted the Mormon Panorama to serve as a witness to history that could teach future generations. Similarly, Christensen intended for his Book of Mormon scenes to function as a witness for the historical nature of the events portrayed. With a strong sense of narrative, a didactic objective, and an effort at detailed accuracy, Christensen's Book of Mormon scenes declare their authenticity. In other words, the images seem to suggest they capture the way ancient events really happened. To convey this visually, Christensen drew on pictorial devices from European academic history painting, Danish Golden Age art, and French Orientalism.

European History Painting's Focus on Narrative

The Church's desire for narrative religious art corresponded to Christensen's own artistic heritage. The legacy of iconoclasm in Lutheran Denmark had resulted in a preference for narrative Bible scenes over iconic images of figures and saints. History paintings—then considered the highest order of painting—undertook subjects from history, myth, and scripture. These paintings were often done in a grand manner with monumental canvases, dramatic action, intense emotions, and a moralizing meaning. History paintings were intended to teach viewers the lessons of history and religion, often in a highly emotional and easily readable way. Following this formula, all ten of Christensen's Book of Mormon scenes consist of narratives told through large figures in action. In the scenes, people are busy traveling, building, preaching, blessing, and working.

Pointing or gesturing figures appear in half of Christensen's series and are a pictorial device he inherited from academic history painters such as Christoffer Wilhelm Eckersberg, who is considered the father of Danish painting. Eckersberg began teaching at the Royal Danish Academy of Fine Arts in 1818 and was director from 1827–1829. He continued to be involved with the school, including reviewing student applications for advanced classes, during the time of Christensen's enrollment. Pointing figures in the art help express the narrative. In *Lehi Preaching to the Jews* (Fig. 3.1), for example, a man on the edge of the crowd points toward Lehi in a mocking gesture. The gestures of other figures in the crowd also help tell the story, as one raises his upturned palm questioningly and one raises his staff in opposition. Additionally, Lehi raises his arm in a traditional rhetorical pose that indicates he is speaking. In *The Building of the Ship* (Fig. 3.2), figures point toward the work being done, a compositional device that leads the

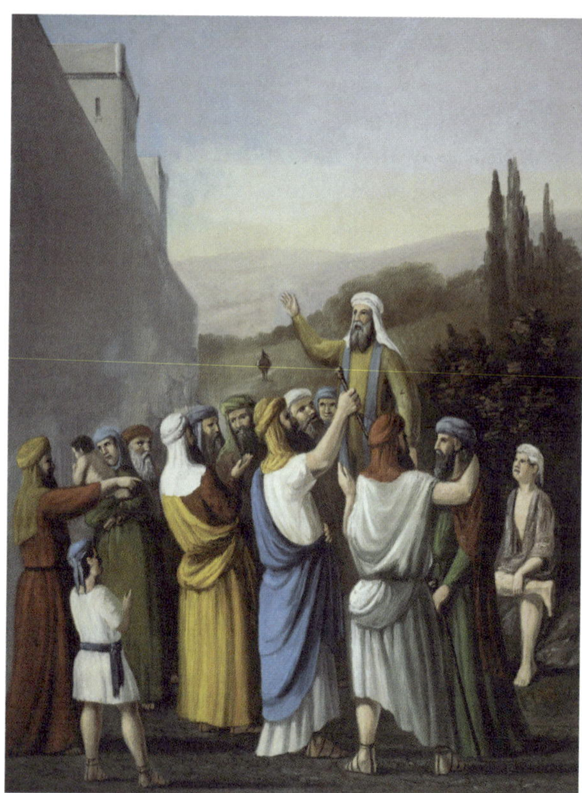

Figure 3.1 C. C. A. Christensen, *Lehi Preaching to the Jews*, c. 1890, oil on composition board, 24¾ × 18⅝ inches, Church History Museum, The Church of Jesus Christ of Latter-day Saints.

viewer's eye into the scene and toward the focal point. Similarly, in *Nephi Making the Plates for the Records* (Fig. 3.3), a dutiful mother directs her child's attention to the work of preserving the record.

Another pictorial device is the symbolic use of color. History paintings traditionally used color as an additional way to help tell the story visually. In Christensen's series, Lehi is shown in a yellow tunic with a blue sash and a white headdress. To easily distinguish Nephi, he always wears a blue tunic with a yellow headdress.

Students still studied and copied history painting when Christensen was training at the Royal Danish Academy in the late 1840s, but it was falling out of fashion due to the rise of portraiture, landscapes, and realistic genre scenes of contemporary life. Yet, by the 1870s, history painting was on the rise again, championed through the work of Carl Bloch and his new mode of Danish history painting. Additionally, in 1878, the Museum of National History at

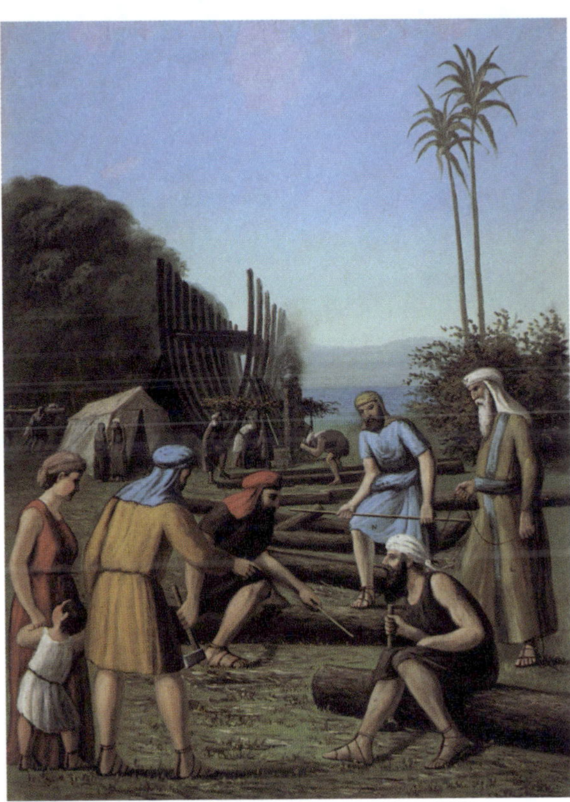

Figure 3.2 C. C. A. Christensen, *The Building of the Ship*, c. 1890, oil on composition board, 24¾ × 18⅝ inches, Church History Museum, The Church of Jesus Christ of Latter-day Saints.

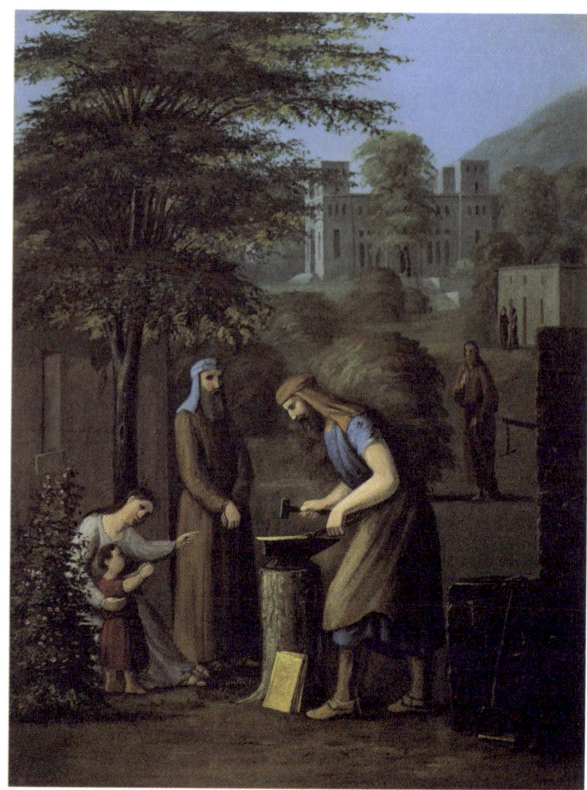

Figure 3.3 C. C. A. Christensen, *Nephi Making the Plates for the Records*, c. 1890, oil on composition board, 24¾ × 18⅝ inches, Church History Museum, The Church of Jesus Christ of Latter-day Saints.

Frederiksborg Castle was opened to display grand history paintings. Scholar Anna Schram Vejlby explained the role of the Museum of National History as "an institution aimed at educating the people through history painting's edifying tales."[7] A decade later, Christensen witnessed this changing Danish style while serving a three-year mission in Scandinavia. As he was mainly stationed at Copenhagen, he recorded that he had many opportunities to visit the Nordic Exhibition of Arts and Industries, where the best Danish painting of the day was exhibited. Christensen also visited Frederiksborg Castle in September 1888 and wrote that he saw Bloch's series of paintings on the life of Christ there and they "interested [him] very much."[8] Just eighteen months later, and less than four months after returning to Utah from his mission, Christensen began his series on the life of Nephi.

Christensen's work echoes many of the elements of Bloch's history painting. Christensen's *Lehi Preaching to the Jews* (see again, Fig. 3.1) and Bloch's

The Sermon on the Mount[9] both include an atmospheric background of a city or landscape that sets the stage for the narrative in the foreground; large, gesturing figures that dominate the canvas; a predominance of primary colors (red, yellow, and blue); and a nod to neoclassical poses, drapery, and architecture. This was a change in style for Christensen. His earlier paintings from the 1870s, such as those in the Mormon Panorama, had many small figures set within a vast landscape, used a variety of colors, and were more in line with the style of early nineteenth-century Danish history painting (see, for example, Fig. 2.11).[10]

In 1890, Christensen chose to work in the new style of history painting exemplified by Bloch, even when his Latter-day Saint contemporaries were going in a different direction. As Noel Carmack has argued, the illustrations by Ottinger, William Armitage, John Held Sr., and William C. Morris in Reynolds's *The Story of the Book of Mormon* in 1888 have more dynamism and are similar to the style of early nineteenth-century American history painters like Benjamin West.[11] Ottinger contributed two pieces to the 1890 Book of Mormon series. As an American who studied at the prestigious Pennsylvania Academy of Fine Arts, Ottinger's approach in these works was in the mode of American academic painting. Christensen's stylistic choices in this series are quite different from Ottinger's and are more like the contemporary Danish history painting of Bloch.

From January to March 1849, Bloch and Christensen were classmates in the first freehand drawing class at the Royal Danish Academy of Fine Arts in Copenhagen.[12] The next year Christensen joined the Church and shifted his attention to reading Mormon scripture and literature, helping his mother and brothers emigrate, and preparing for a mission. As a non-paying, apprenticed student, Christensen was already juggling school with small jobs and could not afford to attend every semester. At least twice, his applications for the Academy's elite live-model classes were rejected by a committee including Eckersberg and Wilhelm Marstrand.[13] Bloch, the son of a merchant, was a paying student and continued attending classes regularly. In 1853, Bloch won the big silver medal at the Royal Danish Academy, and Christensen gave up professional painting to serve a mission. Bloch went on to study in France, Italy, Greece, and the Netherlands before becoming a professor and then vice director at the Royal Danish Academy.

In a twist of fate, Bloch's New Testament art is now more familiar to most Church members than Christensen's Book of Mormon series. Reproductions of Bloch's life of Christ series and other altarpieces adorn Latter-day Saint temples, meetinghouse hallways, and Sunday School manuals.[14] Two of Bloch's works, including the massive *Christ Healing at the Pool of Bethesda*, are owned by the Brigham Young University Museum of Art.

Christensen, who never reached the highest levels of training at the Academy, did not have Bloch's skill in rendering anatomy or composing scenes. But Christensen did know how to tell a story through visual art. In the Book of Mormon series, Christensen's focus on narrative through the use of action, gesture, and symbol relates closely to the didactic purpose of the images. The series was intended to help tell the story of the Book of Mormon and to make it more real in the minds of Church members. This approach was similar to the way mass-produced Bible pictures were used in nineteenth-century America. Indeed, Christensen's images were initially printed alongside a written text in the *Juvenile Instructor*, which directly explained their moralizing meaning. Many of these lessons, written by Reynolds, refer to "the important truth" or "the great truth" that is being taught and include topics such as the knowledge of God, the blessings of obedience, the power of prayer, and the importance of faith.[15] By drawing on the long and venerable tradition of history painting, Christensen set his paintings up as witnesses to history. Through a variety of pictorial devices, including an emphasis on narrative and large active figures, history paintings indicate to the viewer that they document something important in an authoritative way.

Danish Golden Age Naturalism

The Danish Golden Age was a period of artistic flourishing in Denmark between 1800 and 1864. Christensen trained as an artist at the Royal Danish Academy in the 1840s and 1850s, during this remarkable moment. One of the hallmarks of the Danish Golden Age was an interest in adding greater naturalism to visual art. Likewise, throughout the Book of Mormon series—and, in fact, throughout his oeuvre—Christensen incorporated humanizing details observed in real life. This is perhaps especially due to the legacy of Eckersberg, who, through his studies in Paris with Jacques-Louis David and then in Rome with Bertel Thorvaldsen,[16] developed a kind of idealized realism. At the Academy, Eckersberg encouraged students to paint outdoors from nature and to portray scenes of Danish life realized in classical forms. In the Book of Mormon series, Christensen's attention to naturalism is evident in the poses of figures, the careful inclusion of women and children, the indication of the passage of time, and the depiction of the accoutrements of daily life.

As an Academy-trained artist, Christensen certainly sought to emulate neoclassical models in his figures, yet he added a sense of liveliness that made them seem more realistic. His process involved quick sketches from life of real people and scenes. For instance, a pencil sketch in his journal for July–September 1865 captures a scene likely witnessed on his own travels back east before sailing for his second European mission.[17] One figure huddles inside a covered wagon, two men crouch down to repair a wagon wheel or unload supplies, another stands in front of a wagon, while a fifth person sets a kettle above a small fire. In this quick sketch, Christensen captured several natural poses of people in a wagon train. Even more hastily sketched is *Pawnee Camp 28 of June on Platte River Not Far from Columbus*, from the same journal (Fig. 3.4).[18] The focus is on two men in the middle foreground, running with spears raised. To the right, more Pawnee figures are shown in various attitudes of standing or sitting. Behind them, a woman bends forward to point sternly at a child. Several figures in the left background are given the slightest indication by a few strokes of the

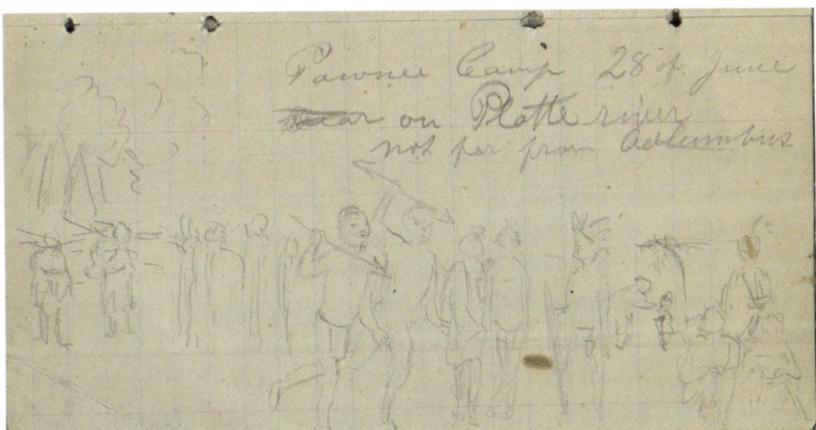

Figure 3.4 C. C. A Christensen, *Pawnee Camp 28 of June on Platte River not far from Columbus*, 1865, pencil drawing on paper, Journal 1865 July–September, Church History Library, The Church of Jesus Christ of Latter-day Saints.

pencil. On this small notebook page, Christensen captured a lively scene of a bustling camp with a variety of figures and poses.

Like the great Danish painter Eckersberg, Christensen naturalized his classical figures. As historians Richard Jensen and Richard Oman observed, Christensen "depended on careful observation of real people for figures in his paintings."[19] They note the pose of the seated boy in *Lehi Preaching to the Jews* (see again, Fig. 3.1) as being different from neoclassical poses and looking instead like a somewhat graceless pose observed in real life. This type of naturalism was a defining element of Danish Golden Age painting. An excellent example is Marstrand's *Church-Goers Arriving by Boat at the Parish Church of Leksand on Siljan Lake, Sweden.*[20] In Marstrand's very large canvas (4¼ × 7 feet), people in a crowd are shown in a variety of natural poses and activities. Near the center, a man balances precariously on an oar while clutching a baby and helping his wife climb backward out of the ship in what is certainly not a classical pose. Nearby, a young mother slouches on a rock nursing her baby. A boy behind her lies on the sand to drink from the lake. These vignettes add variety and a bit of comic naturalism to the monumental scene. Appearing in 1853, the year that Christensen concluded his Royal Danish Academy training and began his first mission in Denmark and Norway, it was immediately popular. The painting was purchased for The Royal Picture Gallery at Christiansborg Palace in Copenhagen, which was open to the public.[21] Christensen likely would have seen it.

Christensen's dedication to naturalism throughout the series is also apparent in the way he indicates the passage of time. This is especially clear in the changing appearances of Lehi and Nephi, the inclusion of women in the later images, and the portrayal of growing children. Throughout the series, Lehi's forked beard becomes progressively whiter. Similarly, Nephi has a youthful, beardless face in the first four scenes but is then portrayed with a dark beard in the second half of the images. In the first five images, the only woman shown is Sariah. But in the later images, we see the daughters of Ishmael, who married Nephi and his brothers, in every one of the five scenes. Children also appear in these later scenes. First, one small toddler is included in *The Building of the Ship* (see again, Fig. 3.2). Then, in *Lehi Blessing His Posterity* (Fig. 3.5), the crowd includes a central figure of a woman nursing a baby while her toddler looks on, and a woman holding an infant in one hand and an older child in the other. Christensen's attention to these small details indicating the passage of time shows his attempt to make the scenes look historically accurate.

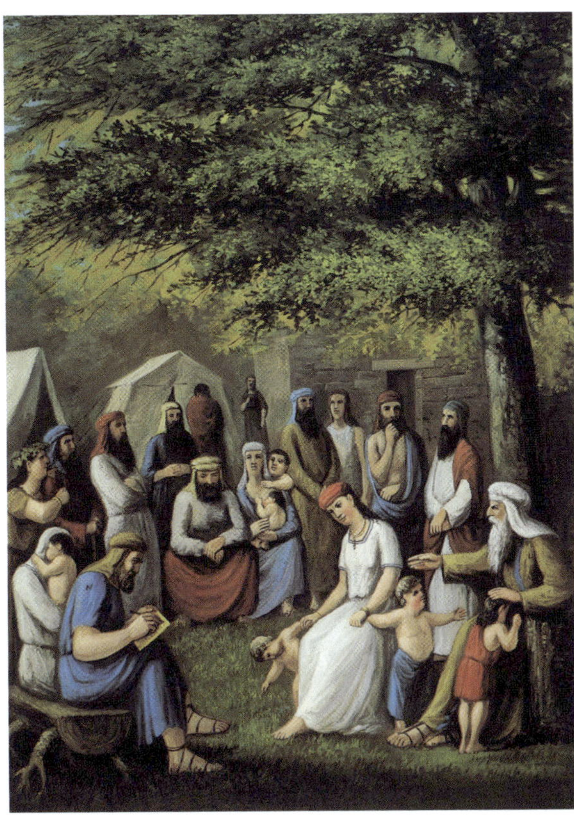

Figure 3.5 C. C. A. Christensen, *Lehi Blessing His Posterity*, c. 1890, oil on composition board, 24¾ × 18⅝ inches, Church History Museum, The Church of Jesus Christ of Latter-day Saints.

Finally, Christensen added realism to the scenes by including a variety of quotidian objects, many of which would have been familiar to his Utah audience. This, too, is similar to the display of contemporary objects in genre scenes of the Danish Golden Age. Leading artists like Eckersberg and Constantin Hansen included detailed renderings of everyday items such as teacups, furniture, pipes, pillows, birdcages, and candlesticks.[22] Similarly, in *Lehi Blessing His Posterity* (see again, Fig. 3.5), several objects of daily life appear. First, two different styles of canvas tents rise behind the extended family. Next to them is a small stone building that looks like common nineteenth-century American buildings. The prominent post and lintel construction of the doorway reveals Christensen's attention to details observed from life. A final charming element is the bench Nephi sits on. It is made of an upturned split log resting on branches. Perhaps this kind of bench was used in Christensen's Utah settlement. Christensen included similar items in *The Building of the Temple*: a clay water jug, ropes and ladders, a wooden cart, and various construction tools. Christensen's use of Danish-style naturalism gave his Book of Mormon paintings an immediacy for his nineteenth-century Utah audience and helped present the images as witnesses to history.

Although Christensen's rise to prominence as a Latter-day Saint artist in the 1870s to 1890s coincided with the rise of Impressionism and modern art in Europe and America, Christensen remained faithful to traditional Danish styles. Claude Monet's *Impression, Sunrise*, which is regarded as the foundational work of the Impressionist movement, was exhibited in Paris at the First Impressionist Exhibition in 1874. By the 1880s, American artists such as Childe Hassam and Mary Cassatt had embraced Impressionism. Whereas academic art valued illusionistic realism, modern art called attention to the materials of paint and canvas and to the mark of the artist. Christensen's art seems to have been unaffected by the new styles. In fact, it is not clear that he was much aware of the European avant-garde during these years. For a period of twenty years, from 1868 to 1887, Christensen did not travel outside of the western Latter-day Saint communities. His mission journals from 1865–1868 and 1887–1889 discuss various visits to Scandinavian art exhibitions (which largely retained a preference for conservative styles), and even a stop at the Museum of Art and Zoology and Antiquity while passing through Liverpool, but there is no record of him visiting American museums.

Whether or not Christensen was aware of new styles moving away from the mores of academic art, he strongly adhered to traditional artistic practices and inclinations he had learned at the Royal Danish Academy of Fine Arts. This remained true even as other successful Latter-day Saint artists in Utah—such as John Hafen, Lorus Pratt, and John B. Fairbanks—embraced Impressionist style and were even sent on a Church-supported mission to Paris in the early 1890s to train in the new techniques.

Christensen's art, like Danish Golden Age art, is representational rather than stylized. He held to his style even while the rise of modern art in Europe and America led to the decline of the Paris Salon by the late 1880s. Closer to home, the Latter-day Saint Paris art missionaries initiated a penchant for Impressionist landscapes in Utah. In a quite different vein, Christensen's art privileged didactic message over aesthetic form. While Hafen and his colleagues created an enduring inclination toward Impressionist landscapes for Latter-day Saint fine artists and patrons, Christensen's art set a tone of mimetic realism for Church-sponsored religious art.

French Orientalism and the Perception of Historical Accuracy

By the time he painted the Book of Mormon series, Christensen had long demonstrated a desire to make his paintings look as historically accurate as possible. His earliest known religious work, the Huntington Panorama, for example, takes pains to visually connect the hillside where Moroni hid the plates and the hillside where Joseph Smith received those same plates (see, Fig. 2.9 and Fig. 2.8). This connection seems to make the images a visual witness of the historical fact of the plates. Likewise, in the Mormon Panorama, Christensen included details based on eyewitness accounts of the events, lending the images an aura of authenticity. In the same way, Christensen used details of costuming, architecture, and environment to create a feeling of historical accuracy in his Book of Mormon paintings. This was likely necessary to comply with the stipulations for the Deseret Sunday School Union contest, which noted,

> The Union desires the artists maintain, as far as possible, the unities of time, place, dress, etc., that the pictures may not be misleading to the children, even in their minor details. The characters therein (except the angels) are all Israelites of the sixth century before Christ, and the localities are Palestine, Arabia and Chili [*sic*].[23]

Regarding this emphasis on accuracy, art historian Nathan Rees argued, a "focus on truthfulness urged Mormon artists and viewers away from hieratic, symbolic images and toward an aesthetic of truth-signaling naturalism."[24] This stress on authenticity and naturalism was not unique to Restoration art, as it was already an established trend in European art and in contemporary American Bible illustrations. No style better exemplified this obsession with creating a feeling of a certain time and place through a veneer of realism than the nineteenth-century French Orientalist art movement.

French Orientalism was an area of academic art related to the styles of Neoclassicism and Romanticism taught at the French Académie des Beaux-Arts. This approach popularized an interest in Middle Eastern topography, dress, and customs, and was evident too in Western literature, music, and fashion. Orientalist images often include palm trees and figures dressed in robes and turbans. Artists drew on nineteenth-century Middle Eastern architecture and costuming to imagine (often inaccurately) how ancient Bible lands looked. The artists used a realistic style and included historical details and objects to give the images a greater sense of (ostensibly) historical veracity. A political or moralizing impulse lies just beneath the veil of exoticism, as the Orient (or East) is typically presented as a foil to the Occident (or West).[25]

Danish art of the mid-nineteenth century was influenced by French Orientalism. Horace Vernet, a leading French Orientalist painter, befriended Danish artist Bertel Thorvaldsen while they were both working in Rome in the early 1830s.[26] Vernet's close friendship with Thorvaldsen—who would return to Denmark to direct the Royal Danish Academy in the years right before Christensen enrolled—likely augmented the influence of his Orientalist style in Danish art.

Orientalism was popular not only in Europe but also in the United States, especially in the years between 1870 and 1900. The American mania for all things Arab and exotic mapped exactly onto the years Christensen was producing images of a Near Eastern family transplanted to the Americas. First, in the early 1870s, Christensen included Book of Mormon scenes in the Huntington Panorama. Then, his 1890 Book of Mormon series, which focused on the life of Nephi, revisited some of these same scenes and added more. In both series, Christensen turned to Orientalizing motifs and careful details as a way of proclaiming the "historicity" of the images.

Art historian Linda Nochlin noted the function of realistic details in Orientalist art: "Such details, supposedly there to denote the real directly, are actually there simply to signify its presence in the work as a whole."[27] In much the same way, Christensen's Book of Mormon images utilize Orientalizing motifs and details but apply them to depictions of ancient America. Christensen was one of many American and European artists at the time transferring Orientalizing motifs to American landscapes and Indigenous figures during the late nineteenth century.[28] Interrogating how Christensen fit into this larger cosmopolitan style reveals his lifelong, active engagement with contemporary European and American art. Moreover, a consideration of Christensen's Orientalizing motifs in Book of Mormon art facilitates a better understanding of Latter-day Saint thought about connections between the Old and New Worlds.

For instance, what are we to make of the many parallels between Christensen's *Nephi Making the Plates for the Records* (see again, Fig. 3.3) and Vernet's *Rebecca and Eliezer*?[29] In both images, two central figures face each other in the foreground next to the central narrative element (the well and trough in Vernet's, the anvil and plates in Christensen's). Additionally, both images have a large tree filling the vertical space on one side. In each image, the other side shows people walking along a pathway that leads to a building. Both artists attempted to clothe the figures in an ancient, exotic style of dress. The special attention given to environment, architecture, and realistic details in these two images underpins their claims to be authoritative representations.

In Vernet's image, the imagined biblical setting is indicated by palm trees, camels, and a city in the distance, along with the belted robes, shawls, sandals, and kaffiyeh worn by the figures. Both images prominently feature a tree that is an important indicator of geographical place. Whereas Vernet has a palm tree to indicate ancient Bible lands, Christensen has a leafy deciduous species to indicate America. In other paintings from the series, such as *The Building of the Ship* (see again, Fig. 3.2), there are prominent palm trees in the Orientalist fashion. To indicate the change in location, Christensen painted only deciduous trees in the remaining scenes, which took place in the promised land of the New World.

Architecture, too, signals the images' claims to authenticity. Vernet included a city based on Middle Eastern models, but Christensen featured the newly built Nephite temple. The building looming up behind Nephi resembles the Manti Temple near Christensen's home, with its rectangular shape, rows of elongated vertical windows, frontal steps, and end towers (but without French mansard cupolas). Dedicated in May of 1888, shortly before Christensen painted this series, the Manti Temple was a point of pride for the Sanpete community. Christensen even painted a Creation Room mural in the Manti Temple in 1886. He had also painted murals in the St. George Temple in 1881, and these were likely the only temples of the Restored Church that Christensen had seen. The Salt Lake Temple was not dedicated until 1893, and there is no record of Christensen visiting the Logan Temple (the only other existing temple at the time). It seems that Christensen looked to the Manti and St. George temples for inspiration in the design of the Nephite temple.

By referencing nineteenth-century Utah temples, Christensen implies a theological, cultural, and perhaps even geographical link between the Great Basin Latter-day Saints and the ancient Nephites. This is an important difference between Christensen and other Orientalist artists. Whereas most Orientalist artists portrayed the people and places of other cultures as less civilized or in need of Western support, Christensen shows these ancient, exotic Nephites as not only righteous but also closely linked to contemporary Western members of the Church. The final image of Nephi making the plates does this most directly, with its inclusion of a temple that echoes the Manti Temple and the metal plates that would become the foundational scripture for the Restored Church.

Finally, both the Christensen and Vernet images rely on the careful depiction of objects to heighten their sense of photographic realism and to help tell the story. Vernet included a rope to pull the water jug up from the well, the bracelet gift Eliezer holds behind his back, the camel trough that Rebecca filled, and Eliezer's traveling partner in the background adjusting the camels' saddles. Even the way in which Rebecca tips forward the water jug while supporting it on her other arm increases the feeling of realism. Rebecca's graceful, partially undraped figure lends an aura of eroticism that was common in Orientalist art. Christensen also added realistic details but, again in a deviation from typical Orientalist art, he combined elements of the ancient past with contemporary details. His painting includes blacksmithing tools that were immediately relatable to nineteenth-century members of the Church and visually linked the two civilizations. In the painting, Nephi is in the guise of a nineteenth-century blacksmith, complete with leather apron, hammer and anvil, tongs and shovel, and forge. Blacksmiths were an essential part of Latter-day Saint settlements in Utah at the time, and inclusion of these familiar elements made the scene accessible for contemporary viewers. It bridged the gap of time and space between the Utah Saints and the Nephites. There is an attention to process here—an interest not just in the fact that Nephi made plates, but in *how* he made them. Nephi is shown as a literal forger of doctrinal truth. The implication is that the artistic process on display in the creation of these paintings likewise comes from a place of authority and accuracy.

Another common theme in Orientalizing art and literature was the romanticized idea of the "last of the race."[30] It shows up in paintings of lone Indigenous figures set within a wild landscape and in stories like the Leatherstocking Tales by James Fenimore Cooper. This theme creeps into both Christensen's 1871 and 1890 Book of Mormon paintings. As readers of the Book of Mormon, his audience knew how the story would end for Nephi's family: with one man left standing, roaming the landscape, and trying to preserve the record of a once-great nation before he dies. This message is made explicit in Christensen's 1871 *Moroni Hiding the Plates* from the Huntington Panorama (see again, Fig. 2.9), showing the wounded Mormon handing off the metal record to his son, Moroni, who will be the last Nephite. *Nephi Making the Plates for the Records* (see again, Fig. 3.3) also hints at the need to preserve the beliefs and history of a people that will die out. This same story was playing out in real time with the Indigenous people of the Utah territory where Christensen lived.

Christensen was certainly not alone in turning to a picturesque, exotic style in his Book of Mormon paintings. The Orientalist craze swept through European and American art in the late nineteenth century. Christensen's inclusion of so many Orientalizing motifs—attention to clothing, flora, architecture, realistic details, and romantic ideas of a dying but beautiful civilization—indicates his continuing engagement with broader trends in Western, and especially Danish, art. These motifs also expose a certain political outlook that saw European settlers in America as the rightful inheritors of the land. Just as French Orientalist art supported the European domination of North African regions, even while it celebrated the culture of the dwindling native Arab population, so too did Christensen's Book of Mormon series proclaim the place of nineteenth-century Church members in Utah, while memorializing the history of the shrinking Indigenous population.

A New Vision: Art as a Witness to Doctrine

Christensen's Book of Mormon paintings follow patterns of nineteenth-century European art in their focus on narrative and didacticism, their inclusion of humanizing details, and their attempt at historical accuracy. In these ways, the art aims to proclaim its authenticity as a witness to past events. At the same time, the art serves as a witness to ongoing Church doctrine. In particular, the visual devices and symbols used in this series reveal an early Latter-day Saint understanding of divine embodiment and of the role of God's chosen people.

Divine Embodiment

Building on centuries of religious iconography, early Latter-day Saint artists turned to European precedent to visually depict Book of Mormon content and make the artworks intelligible to viewers. In doing so, they also had to be careful to distinguish beliefs peculiar to their Church. The visual devices Christensen used to portray scenes from the life of Nephi worked well to imagine what real events may have looked like. But these same devices did not work as well to depict a heaven-sent vision. Thus, the most striking image in the series is *Nephi's Vision of the Virgin and Child* (Fig. 3.6). Christensen's understanding of and contribution to Latter-day Saint thought about divine embodiment is expressed in this painting through the angel's use of narrative gesture, his lack of wings or traditional iconography, his grounding, and his white robe.

A highlight of Nephi's account of the vision in 1 Nephi 11 is his prophetic view of the nativity of Christ. Christensen's depiction of the Christ child with his mother Mary echoes that of countless European paintings. This icon-like portrayal of Mary and Christ is surprisingly Catholic in style for a Lutheran-turned-Baptist-turned-Mormon artist. Mary appears in her traditional blue robe, symbolizing her role as heavenly queen. She

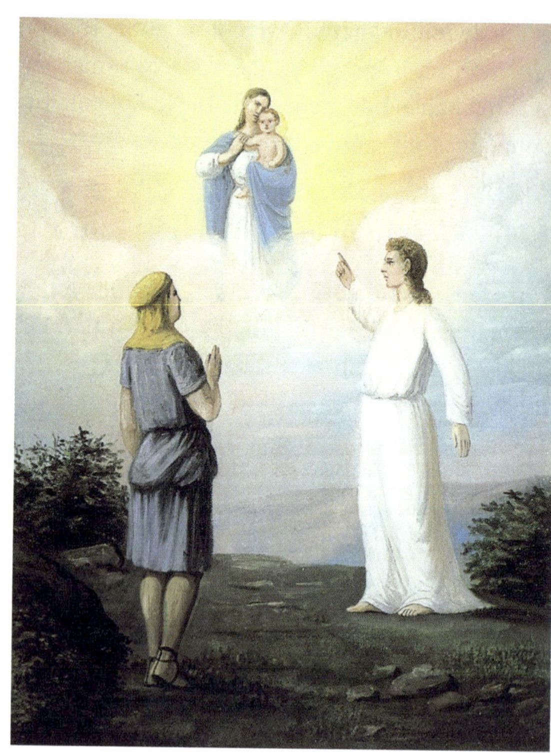

Figure 3.6 C. C. A. Christensen, *Nephi's Vision of the Virgin and Child*, c. 1890, oil on composition board, 24¾ × 18⅝ inches, Church History Museum, The Church of Jesus Christ of Latter-day Saints.

is depicted as the *Theotokos*, or God-bearer, as she holds the child in her arms. The composition is borrowed from John Held Sr.'s *Vision of Nephi*[31] published in *The Story of the Book of Mormon*. As scholar Noel Carmack has suggested, Held, as perhaps the first to visualize this scene, was "turning to familiar religious imagery" from Europe.[32] Held immigrated to Utah from Switzerland when he was only eight years old, and later studied art at the University of Utah, where he would have become familiar with the classics of Renaissance and Baroque art. He did not return to Europe, and he was not steeped in European Protestant art and culture the way that Christensen was. Perhaps this explains why he was more comfortable turning to traditional Catholic iconography for his *Vision of Nephi*. Thus, Christensen's painting of Nephi's Vision, which is copied heavily from Held's composition, feels somewhat out of place among his other images that are more influenced by the Danish style of narrative realism.

The iconic image of the Madonna and Child in clouds can be found throughout the works of Renaissance and Baroque artists, including Donatello, Raphael, Parmigianino, Rembrandt, and Murillo. Raphael's *Sistine Madonna* (c. 1512–1514) was particularly influential.[33] In Raphael's painting, which is quite similar to Christensen's, Mary wears a blue robe and holds the Christ child up close to her face. She stands in a classical contrapposto stance on a cloud, flanked by Pope Sixtus II and Saint Barbara. Light emanates from her idealized figure.

Latter-day Saints veered sharply from the Catholic and Orthodox use of icons, or images seen not just as symbols of the divine but as objects of veneration themselves. While Held and Christensen looked to traditional renderings of the Virgin and Child on a cloud, they both worked to prevent the scene from becoming an icon by adding the narrative element of "an angel" from heaven pointing out the vision to Nephi.[34] Christensen even added the additional narrative gesture of Nephi's hand raised in awe. The narrative gesture puts the image squarely back in the realm of didactic history painting.

Despite a reliance on European compositions for the Virgin and Child, the depiction of the angel by Christensen indicates an attempt to fashion a new Latter-day Saint iconography. This is especially clear in the way the angel is portrayed with a physical body and without wings, which was a radical break from traditional Christian iconography. English professor Edgar Garcia has noted similar complexities in seeking to visualize another Book of Mormon angel, Moroni. If the Book of Mormon teaches that Moroni was an Indigenous American Nephite, Garcia explains, then Moroni,

> should not look like the commonplace angels of European Christian iconography. He shouldn't be so white, so appropriate to a painting by Giotto or Michelangelo, should he? While not actually white, he also shouldn't be Thomistic, that is, with a type of angelic *form* (one must not say body) set forth by the great doctor of angelology Thomas Aquinas: to wit, incorporeal, completely spiritual, purely intellectual, and inclined to thoughts and behavior profoundly alien to human beings. Unlike these angelic types, Moroni is provocatively embodied; and what provokes about his body is its location in space, time, and history.[35]

It is precisely this type of portrayed embodiment that makes Christensen's angel unique for the time. Unlike traditional depictions of angels, his angel is not only wingless but also has its feet firmly planted on the ground. The heavenly messenger's long, heavy robes pool around his bare feet. The fact of his material, literal presence is further highlighted by his positioning on the same sharply rendered patch of *terra firma* as Nephi, separate from the space occupied by the ethereal vision, which is painted in lighter pastels. This weighty figure stands in contrast to Christensen's earlier portrayal of the hovering angel Moroni in *The Hill Cumorah* from the Mormon Panorama, suggesting that over time, Christensen was experimenting with developing a new Latter-day Saint visual vocabulary. Richard Oman has observed that even Christensen's earlier angel Moroni, with his mature, bearded face but lack of wings, was significantly different from the way in which angels had been portrayed in European art and would have a lasting effect on the portrayal of angels in Latter-day Saint art.[36] Perhaps Christensen was also responding to George Q. Cannon's recent condemnation of art showing angels with wings.[37]

Although the white robe of Christensen's angel parallels the white robes on angels in many European paintings, it also references a theological point that Christensen gave some thought to while on his third mission. In 1888, he published a sermon titled "The Immortality of the Soul" in both *Skandinaviens Stjerne* in Denmark and *Bikuben* in Utah. In this essay, Christensen hypothesized that spirits cross from mortality to immortality unclothed, in the same way that they come to earth at birth. Drawing on Revelation

6:9–11, Christensen mused that white robes are immediately given to these spirits by friends who have already crossed over. In the same sermon, Christensen pointed to Nephi's vision of Mary as evidence for earthly roles being chosen or pre-assigned before birth.[38] The scene described in 1 Nephi 11 was on Christensen's mind around the time he painted this series. And, from his essay, it seems he thought about it principally in terms of questions of embodiment: What does a spirit look like after separating from the mortal body? How might it be clothed in real fabric? and How might the earthly lives of individuals be related to their premortal existence and the assignments given to them? Christensen's interest in these topics reflects a preoccupation among early Latter-day Saints with issues of embodiment and with defining humanity's relation to the divine. After all, the Restoration itself hinged on Joseph Smith's revolutionary claim to have seen God the Father and Jesus Christ as two separate, embodied, living beings. This presented a distinctly different way of understanding the nature of God, and it is reflected in Christensen's art.

Christensen may have modeled his angel after European types, but he made several alterations. He changed the traditional angelic iconographic blessing gesture to a narrative pointing gesture, he removed the old symbols of wings and lilies and rays of light, he put the angel on the ground rather than on a cloud, and he clothed the angel in white. In all these ways, Christensen signaled the literal, material presence of the angel as an embodied figure occupying the same space as Nephi in a particular moment in history. The vision of the Virgin and Child, however, was just a vision—a vision of people that had not even been born on earth yet—and not a literal presence, and so Christensen felt comfortable retaining the old iconography to portray Mary and Jesus. This distinguished the vision from the real world. But in portraying an embodied angel, Christensen was developing a new visual vocabulary for unique Latter-day Saint doctrine and thought.

A Chosen People

Christensen's Book of Mormon series not only demonstrates unique Latter-day Saint ideas about the nature of God, but also about the way that God relates to human beings. The images repeatedly show groups of people trying to work together and follow God's commands. The overarching narrative of the series is one of righteous people being led by God to a safe place where they can worship him freely. Christensen had already explored this Exodus theme in detail in his emotionally charged Mormon Panorama, depicting scenes of persecution and providence in the early history of the Church. He now emphasized a similar theme in the story of Lehi's removal from Jerusalem and arrival in the Promised Land. Christensen's own thinking about religious and political freedom and about how to build a virtuous society is apparent in his depictions of the Nephite experience.

Righteous governance and religious freedom were recurring concerns for Christensen in both his art and his writing. During his third Scandinavian mission, he recorded an 1888 visit to the crypt of the castle of Sønderborg, where Danish monarchs were buried. He reflected on the ways that these monarchs abused their power, writing, "The Grandparents of the present king of Denmark are resting here, and I brought with me some little of the ragged velvet remaining on the outside coffins. Many thoughts crossed my mind, as I gazed upon these silent historical witnesses of past human greatness and power, too often abused."[39] Two days after he arrived home in Utah in November 1889, he remarked in his journal on a talk by a Latter-day Saint leader at a conference in Moroni, Utah, on the topic of righteous governance. Christensen wrote: "I listened to a most soul-stirring discourse of Apostle Moses Thatcher in the afternoon; the subject was 'Confidence' and how to establish between the people and their leaders— he showed, that it was only possible, by gaining the affection of the people, that rulers could govern in righteousness and with success. It brought tears to my eyes."[40]

Christensen may have felt a special concern for religious persecution since he experienced it himself in Norway, where he was imprisoned in both 1853 and 1857 for preaching during his first mission, and in America, where he was arrested in 1889 for unlawful cohabitation. His trial in Provo lasted more than a year. Of the first day in court on November 30, 1889, he wrote in his journal, "This took place on the anniversary of my wedding with my second wife, 21 years ago, an act, which Congress has since made a crime by law and for which I am now made to suffer. But they can only imprison the body—the soul is free to love and honor my wife who has faithfully and patiently shared sorrow and joy with me, during these many years, and raised a family of good and noble children."[41] It was in the early months of these proceedings that Christensen, released on bond, painted his Book of Mormon series.

These paintings by Christensen stand as a visual witness against persecution for belief and unrighteous governance. Just as Latter-day Saints saw their westward journey as a kind of reenactment of the Israelite Exodus, Christensen likely saw parallels between Lehi's experiences and his own. Lehi standing on a street corner preaching to a threatening crowd in *Lehi Preaching to the Jews* (see again, Fig. 3.1) was an experience Christensen was familiar with from his missions. Christensen and his family left their homeland in search of religious liberty and an opportunity to build a Zion society, just like the figures in *Lehi's Family Leaving Jerusalem* (see again, Fig. 2.2). That kind of society, ruled by a wise and righteous patriarch, is exemplified in *Lehi Blessing His Posterity* (see again, Fig. 3.5). In this image, set in a pastoral landscape, Lehi's family appears unified in their purpose of following God. The outstretched, blessing hands of Lehi visually echo the broad leafy branches of the tree springing up from behind him. The tree covers the group as a sort of naturalized cloth of honor, indicating the group's protection and status as a people chosen by God. The scene stands in stark contrast to the next one, *The Separation of the Nephites and Lamanites*, where religious persecution has created the need to once again escape to freedom.

Christensen delights in the scenes that show the people working together to build the kingdom of their God. In *The Building of the Ship* (see again, Fig. 3.2) and *The Building of the Temple*, there is an attention to process, tools, workmanship, and design. The ship scene depicts a variety of jobs: Lehi measuring materials, others preparing to cut wooden beams into planks, men carrying in additional timber. The frame of the ship rises in the background, constructed in the frame-first style of wooden ships in the nineteenth century. Smoke rises from a hearth next to the ship, perhaps alluding to the steam bending technique used to curve the large frame pieces.[42] These scenes align with Christensen's writings about God as the supreme designer who imparts wisdom and design knowledge to his people.

In a series of articles in *Bikuben* in 1892, Christensen pondered the function of art and the divine creative spark found in man. He wrote that God is an artist, gardener, astronomer, geologist, botanist, physician, and architect.[43] Christensen postulated that Enoch must have been taught art and science by God in order to have built a city that could be taken directly into the divine realm.[44] He went on to say that training and skill are required to build the Kingdom of God both on earth and in heaven, and that each member of the Church has their own gifts to contribute to the project. Some people are gifted in science, or trade, or agriculture, and others "endowed . . . as architects, engineers, speakers, statesmen, poets, and artists."[45] In these ways, Christensen implored, members of the Church could work together to build the kind of free, righteous community they longed for.

Conclusions

Nineteenth-century Latter-day Saint artists, such as Christensen, started with existing styles and motifs and adapted them to fit new purposes, messages, and scriptures. Christensen studied the work of European artists and incorporated their approaches in his Book of Mormon paintings. His use of strong narrative elements—such as symbolic colors, action and movement, and gestures—follows the established formula for European history painting. Christensen's interest in naturalizing the figures was inherited from Danish Golden Age painting. His incorporation of details and exotic ancient Near Eastern elements that create an aura of historicity was directly influenced by the artwork of French Orientalists.

Yet, while Christensen drew from these European sources, he found ways to incorporate new iconography and theology. Building on the artwork of John Held Sr., Christensen's depiction of the angel in *Nephi's Vision of the Virgin and Child* is something entirely new, and it set a standard for Latter-day Saint depictions of angels. With this embodied angel, Christensen was able to visualize Latter-day Saint beliefs about the material, living, immanent nature of the divine. Christensen's journals and writings often talk of discovering and teaching "Truth," and this approach carried over to his artistic methods.[46] With their attention to narrative and realistic detail, and their inventive new iconography, Christensen's Book of Mormon paintings were used by the Church as witnesses to the historical truth of scripture and to the veracity of doctrine.

Today, the Church continues to primarily use straightforward, realistic-looking images to teach doctrines and to witness to historical truth. In Church publications, figurative art is heavily favored over abstract or nonrepresentational art. Christensen's 1890 Book of Mormon series, which was distributed by the Deseret Sunday School Union as a flipchart of lithographs, was among only a small handful of images about the Book of Mormon for sixty years. As such, it helped set an enduring expectation for didactic, mimetic religious art. But Christensen's series did more than help shape Latter-day Saint aesthetic style. It helped shape the Latter-day Saint identity as God's chosen people. In a fortuitous—or perhaps brilliant—stroke, Christensen used motifs of Old World art in a New World context to visualize the Book of Mormon's message of restoration. A chosen family leaves Jerusalem at God's bidding, preserves the sacred records, is transplanted to a promised land, builds a righteous community, and passes on their beliefs to future generations. It is not hard to see how Christensen, like other Great Basin Latter-day Saint immigrants, saw their own experiences as a retelling of this ancient story about God's chosen people. The paintings themselves take part in this work of restoration, bringing together the old and the new.

CHAPTER FOUR

Envisioning Zion

Blending Scandinavian, American, and Mormon Identities

With some overlap, Christensen's art and writing fall into three chronological periods, in each of which members of The Church of Jesus Christ of Latter-day Saints are depicted differently in their relationship to other people. Looking at these periods sequentially can help reveal the evolution of Christensen's sense of identity. In the 1850s through 1880s, Christensen was focused on a kind of Latter-day Saint particularity that stood in contrast to contemporary European and American communities. In the 1890s, a shift appeared in Christensen's art that positioned the Sanpete settlers as more like other Americans, and it often did so by using Indigenous people as a foil to the Latter-day Saints. In the early twentieth century, a marked nostalgia for Scandinavian people, places, languages, and customs permeated Christensen's work. As the broader cultural context changed, Christensen's fluid sense of community shifted from a focus on Latter-day Saint peculiarity to an embrace of popular American ideals and images and finally to a concern for Scandinavian heritage.

This gradual change echoes similar shifts in Mormon thought from the mid-nineteenth century to the early twentieth century. Christensen arrived in the Salt Lake Valley by handcart on September 13, 1857, ten years after Brigham Young and the first Latter-day Saint settlers arrived. It was also just days after the Mountain Meadows Massacre. It was a moment of upheaval for the Latter-day Saints as 2,500 federal troops closed in on Salt Lake City. President James Buchanan sent the soldiers to assist in replacing Brigham Young as Utah territorial governor with the federally appointed Alfred Cumming. Young and members of the Church responded by calling up their militia, halting trade with outsiders, blocking army supply lines, and preparing for battle. The standoff, known as the Utah War, lasted through the winter until Cumming was installed in June 1858.

The Utah War revived old fears as the settlers worried about a return of persecutions and what they saw as encroachments on their religious liberty and political sovereignty. Christensen arrived at the height of these tensions, when the moment of Mormon isolation was ending. Christensen had not witnessed the earlier raids in Missouri. Nor had he been forced out of Nauvoo in the winter snow. Yet in this period of renewed anxiety, he heard stories from fellow Saints who had survived these ordeals. Now a member of this Latter-day Saint community, Christensen adopted their history as his own cultural heritage, and he painted it dramatically. To show the contrast between Utah Saints and other Americans, Christensen painted scenes of violent persecution aimed at Latter-day Saints as well as peaceful scenes of successful Utah settlements existing outside the bounds of federal governing structures.

In the late nineteenth century, amid questions of polygamy and Utah statehood, Latter-day Saints adopted a different posture toward America. The Great Basin settlements were now within United States territory and, thanks to the completion of the transcontinental railroad in 1869, were no longer geographically isolated. A series of federal legislation and legal cases aimed at polygamy—including the 1879 *Reynolds v. United States* decision by the Supreme Court and the 1887 Edmunds-Tucker Act—disrupted Latter-day Saint practices and communities. In 1890, Church President Wilford Woodruff declared that the Church no longer taught polygamy nor performed plural marriages. Moreover, Woodruff announced, he would submit to United States laws forbidding plural marriage and "use my influence with the members of the Church over which I preside to have them do likewise."[1] The resolution indicated the Church leader's willingness to accept the terms of American citizenship. As historian Matthew Bowman puts it, at the turn of the twentieth century, the Latter-day Saint task "became assimilation, finding ways to translate the things America demanded of them into the language and imperatives of their own faith."[2] It was in this new era that Christensen painted two views of the Manti Temple that presented the Latter-day Saints as civilized, industrious Americans.

At the dawn of the twentieth century, the Latter-day Saints repurposed their culture of utopian kingdom building by more fully embracing American values and religious pluralism. The impetus was no longer an imminent apocalypse but rather a need to build a sustainable future. Utah was now a state of the Union and not as secluded in its politics, economy, or culture. Yet pockets of Utah, including areas settled by Scandinavian immigrants in Sanpete and Emery Counties, remained relatively insular and loyal to their native heritage. Indeed, the ethnic homogeneity of these areas largely remains today. During the early 1900s—the last decade of Christensen's life—he turned with full purpose to memorializing his Scandinavian identity in both text and paint.

Utah Settlers

Christensen's early writing and art celebrated leaving the old world behind and building Zion in a new country. In his poems and journals, he bemoaned the fate of those who stayed in Babylon (meaning Europe, but also any society not built on the Restored Gospel of Jesus Christ). In the summer of 1853, in Denmark, while helping J. M. Bohn prepare a Danish hymnbook, Christensen penned his first poem, which is full of millenarian fervor and admonitions to serve God and leave Babylon behind. It was included in the early Danish hymnbook as "Lovpriser vor Frelser med Jubel og Sang (Praise to Our Savior with Jubilee and Song)." Translated into English, the third verse reads,

> O Friends, see this is the Savior's command,
> And if you obey Him you will be led out
> Of Babylon's confusion, which soon will fall down:
> O make use of the time, hear the Savior's call.[3]

In the mid-nineteenth century, Latter-day Saints vocalized their desire to separate from "gentiles." Speaking in the fall of 1857, just after Christensen arrived in Utah, Latter-day Saint leader John Taylor declared that his people were persecuted "because we believe in the establishment of the kingdom of God upon the earth . . . because the principles of righteousness are introduced among the children of men, and they expose the evils, corruption, priestcraft, political craft, and the abominations that everywhere exist."[4] Christensen's early writing and painting express this desire to leave Babylon and create a new Latter-day Saint identity that superseded prior ethnic or national claims. Aboard the ship that carried him from Denmark to the United States in 1857, Christensen wrote the poem, "Handcart Song from 1857." Written before he had ever set his own hand to a cart, the poem exudes a sense of optimism, duty, and adventure. With no mention of the old country, the poem looks forward to the new "home" in Salt Lake City, where they will be "free as a bee":

> Come, brethren, let us all gladly
> Go together to Salt Lake City,
> And if we get tired, don't be faint-hearted;
> Spit in your fist, and that's all there is to it.
> We're going to our beloved home,
> Always forward. Dulidulidu.
> And if it seems a little hard, still we can take it.
> The handcart does feel strange and new,
> It is true, from one view;
> But every fellow in some way
> Will take hold better every day
> Till in the end it goes right neatly,
> Doesn't it? Dulidulidu.
> And even if it seems a little hard, we can take it.
>
> Come, my follower and friend!
> Our trip is now almost at an end.
> We are free as a bee.
> Now we quickly hurry on
> Toward our joyful home—dulidulidu—
> And even if it was a little hard,
> We could take it.[5]

Christensen, like most other nineteenth-century Mormon converts in Scandinavia, came from an economically disadvantaged community. Historian Julie Allen noted that, although immigration to Utah may have been religiously motivated, it was also a way to escape the archaic Danish class system and to find greater economic opportunities.[6] According to historians Reid Neilson and Scott Marianno, almost half of Danish immigrants to America at this time came from the working class.[7] The economic impulse was likely a factor for Christensen, his mother, and his brothers in their conversion and emigration in the 1850s. Even in 1868, during his second mission in Norway, Christensen wrote to his mission leader, President Franklin D. Richards,

> The signs of the times here are hunger, sickness, shipwrecks, and a prospect of hard times coming. Thousands are preparing to leave this

> miserable country for America, thereby hoping to escape the threatening evil; and I believe that there is no other people who cherish such a general desire to leave their native land, as do the Norwegians; it is therefore a matter of course, that the Saints here are as anxious to emigrate as anybody.[8]

Many Scandinavian Latter-day Saints of the nineteenth century were not only changing their religious beliefs but also seeking new opportunities under different political and economic systems. This forward-thinking, nation-building mindset appears in another Christensen poem in an early Danish Latter-day Saint hymnal. In it, he contrasted the Saints gathering in Utah with unrighteous people of the past and present. It concluded with the lines:

> In Ephraim's Land in the far West
> Shall beautiful peace be celebrated
> And the children of the covenant far and near
> Will find the Lord's Zion there.[9]

Christensen also looked toward Zion in his visual art. His first paintings in Utah were idealized views of newly built Latter-day Saint homes and settlements, especially those in his beloved Sanpete Valley. Intriguingly, Christensen drew on his Danish art training to depict his new homeland. In a study of nineteenth-century Scandinavia, Allen pointed out that, "like [Christen] Dalsgaard and [Carl] Bloch, Christensen's style . . . reflects the preoccupations of Danish realist painting, with the difference in Christensen's case that his painterly gaze was 'directed not toward Denmark but rather toward the Mormon experience.'"[10]

His early painting *Home! Sweet Home!* (Fig. 4.1) exemplifies this style with its attention to detail and its emphasis on common working people and rural landscapes. A neatly built home takes center stage in the scene, amid emblems of industry and providence: a blooming orchard, a split-rail fence, chickens, and the modest woman of the house going about her daily labors. Highlighted in front of the house, two girls and two boys and the family dog play together. This is the kind of life that called to poor Scandinavians—a place where honest hard work could build a thriving family and homestead. Repeatedly in his poetry too, Christensen lauded the merits of a home built on faith, love, and work.

Of course, the actual story of Utah domestic life was more complicated than it appears in this scene. When this was painted in 1875, Christensen had two wives living in two separate households. It is difficult to determine

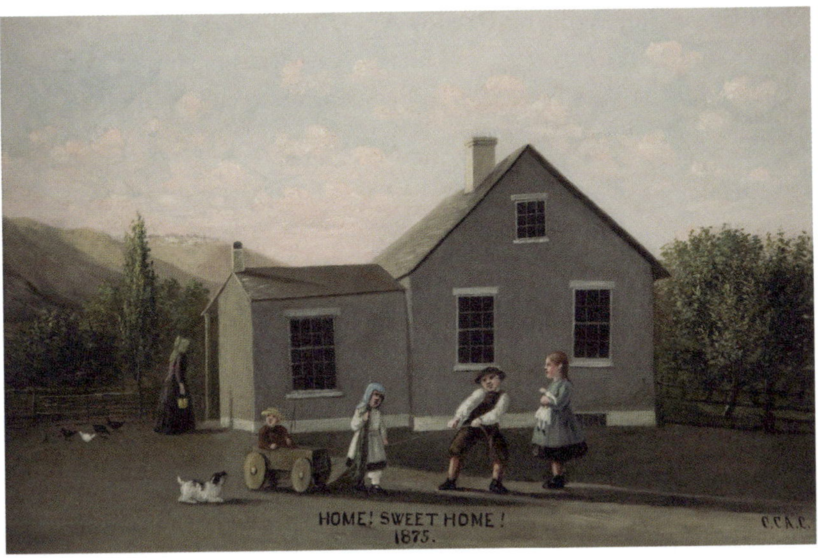

Figure 4.1 C. C. A. Christensen, *Home! Sweet Home!*, 1875, oil on panel, 12¼ × 18½ inches, from the Utah Museum of Fine Arts Permanent Collection, gift of Mr. and Mrs. Joseph J. Palmer.

which wife and children might be shown in this painting. In June of 1875, his second wife, Mary, delivered her fourth baby and first boy after losing her infant third child the previous fall. His first wife, Elise, had seven children, the oldest of whom was sixteen years old at this point. Perhaps the painting depicts another family or is simply a fanciful vision of home life.

While Christensen threw himself into the work of building Zion, many Americans back in "Babylon" were only too happy to mark boundaries between themselves and the Mormons. Latter-day Saints were seen as outside the norms of identity in at least four ways: they were considered unlike other Americans in their theocracy, distinct from other Christians in their theology, unique among Western civilizations in their polygamy, and different from other whites in their ethnicity or race. Often, in rhetoric and political cartoons of the time, this so-called racial difference was a shorthand to mark all the ways in which Mormons were "other." In his study of the racialization of Mormon identity, W. Paul Reeve showed that, from the earliest years of the Church's existence, Americans described Mormons as racially strange, even though most early converts were white Americans or immigrants from Scandinavia and Great Britain.[11] Historian J. Spencer

Fluhman, also analyzing nineteenth-century anti-Mormon rhetoric, similarly examined how, in word and image, Americans portrayed Mormons as non-white barbarians who were "religiously and culturally alien."[12]

Indigenous Neighbors

Questions of race became particularly thorny when considering Latter-day Saint relationships with Utah's Indigenous people. Utah settler relations with local Indigenous populations fluctuated between periods of cautious friendliness, small skirmishes, and outright hostility. Good relationships were desirable out of immediate necessity and because of early Latter-day Saint beliefs in the strong connection between Native Americans and the Lamanites of the Book of Mormon. Thus, at times, the Saints made significant attempts at working with and even baptizing the Potawatomi in Missouri, the Sauk (or Sak) and Meskwaki (or Fox) people near Nauvoo, and later the Ute, Paiute, Goshute, Shoshone, and others in Utah territory. Yet, cultural differences, the enforcement of United States policies, and the amount of water and land needed to sustain the growing Latter-day Saint population led to clashes with Indigenous communities.

Complicating this history were American ideas about Indigenous inferiority and savagery (the Indian Removal Act had been in place since 1830) and fears of a Mormon-Native alliance. As the nineteenth century ended and the Saints worked toward American assimilation, they proffered a narrative of themselves as the pillars of civilization in the American West. This identity relied on the juxtaposition of the modern Saints with the native inhabitants of the past. Christensen's art spanned these time periods and reflected the changing Latter-day Saint attitude toward their Indigenous neighbors.

Christensen's first depiction of Indigenous people was the 1865 pencil sketch of a Pawnee camp in his mission journal (see again, Fig. 3.4). Although the two foreground figures carry spears, the group appears generally peaceful. Christensen's interest in recording the Pawnee is intriguing because he began this mission just as tensions between the Sanpete settlers and the Utes were mounting. Both settlers and Utes were killed in clashes between 1865 and 1872, collectively known as the Black Hawk War. While he was overseas, Christensen's family lost cattle to Ute bands and fled from their home in Mount Pleasant.[13] By 1872, most Utes in central Utah had been relocated by federal agents to the Uintah Reservation, often with the cooperation of Latter-day Saints.[14]

In the northern part of the state, some Church members worked closely with the Shoshone to teach Latter-day Saint beliefs, farming, and American customs. George Washington Hill and Dimick Huntington served as translators and proselyting missionaries to Native Americans from the 1850s through the 1870s. In 1873, Brigham Young officially called Hill to be a missionary to the Shoshone and to teach them to farm.[15] In the spring of that year, Hill baptized hundreds of Shoshone, including Chief Sagwitch.[16] In February of 1875, Sagwitch and his wife were endowed and sealed in the Salt Lake Endowment House by Wilford Woodruff.[17] By the summer of that year, Hill reported that 2,000 Native Americans had been baptized.[18] Hill worked throughout the 1870s to establish a farm run by the Shoshone, first trying a spot near Franklin, Idaho and then spending several years working to develop areas near the Bear and Malad rivers, before finally creating Washakie (near Portage, Utah) in 1880.[19]

At some point in the early 1870s, Huntington commissioned Christensen to paint a scroll as an aid in teaching Native people. The scroll's eleven scenes (listed in chapter two) illustrated events from the Bible and Book of Mormon, beginning with Adam and Eve and ending with Moroni handing the plates to Joseph Smith. In March of 1875, Frederick Kesler recorded that he saw this panorama exhibited and explained to a gathering of Native Americans in Salt Lake City with Brigham Young and other Church leaders.[20] Hill's daughter-in-law recounted that when Huntington died in 1879, the scroll was given to Hill. She remembered seeing him use the scroll with "nice large pictures of the different Nephites and different leaders" as he talked to Native Americans and "told them about their forefathers."[21]

Although Christensen did not paint contemporary Shoshone or Utes in this panorama, he and other Latter-day Saints at the time believed these nations to be descended from the Israelite family depicted. While this belief led Church members to feel a special affinity with Native Americans, the European American settlers nevertheless harbored the widely accepted view at the time that Indigenous society was less civilized than their own and in need of reform.[22] For the Saints, then, teaching Native Americans to live and act and believe as they did was a key element of the redemption of mankind.

This view is visually expressed in Christensen's *Joseph Preaching to the Indians* (Fig. 4.2), painted a few years later, in the late 1870s, in his

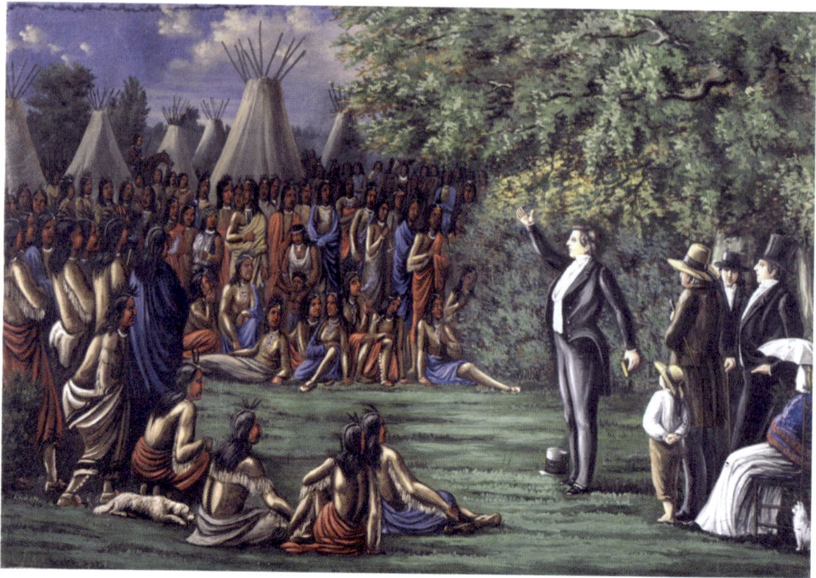

Figure 4.2 C. C. A. Christensen, *Joseph Preaching to the Indians*, c. 1878, tempera on muslin, 76½ × 112¾ inches. Brigham Young University Museum of Art, gift of the grandchildren of C. C. A. Christensen, 1970.

Mormon Panorama. He based his composition on an 1843 lithograph by British artist John McGahey, who traveled throughout the American West with fellow artist George Catlin.[23] The image captures a scene from August 12, 1841, described by Joseph Smith in his dictated history. Smith recorded that he spoke, through an interpreter, with "a considerable number of the Sac and Fox Indians" about the Book of Mormon and urged them to peace.[24] In an analysis of Christensen's painting, Laura Hurtado and David Grua describe how McGahey and Catlin worried about the United States' treatment of Native nations and appreciated Latter-day Saint efforts to befriend the tribes. Hurtado and Grua see in both McGahey's and Christensen's images an attempt to heroize "Smith as the ultimate champion of a marginalized people."[25] The image visually contrasts the finely dressed Saints with the Native Americans, many of whom sit on the ground. The message is that Joseph Smith brings culture, peace, and religion to a "primitive" people.

It would be ten years before Christensen painted Indigenous figures again. Perhaps, as the Utah settlers looked to align themselves with popular

American messages in the 1880s and 1890s, it was considered best to avoid illustrating friendly associations between the Latter-day Saints and the tribes. Reeve details long-standing national concerns about such friendships, including rumors that "Mormons in their actions and characteristics assumed the identity of Indians, Mormons were intent upon forging Indian alliances to overthrow white America, and . . . Mormons entered into racially regressive marriages with Indians."[26] In national rhetoric, the Latter-day Saints were often conflated with Indigenous people and sometimes called "white Indians."[27] To prove their Americanness, Latter-day Saints had to show they were different from their Indigenous neighbors. In the 1890s, Christensen included Indigenous people in three of his monumental artistic projects: the Hancock Panorama, *Temple Hill in Manti, November 1849*, and *The Handcart Company*. In all three, the native people are shown as either violent, threatening, or culturally inferior to the white settlers. The images are in striking contrast to the peaceful grouping of families in the earlier *Joseph Preaching to the Indians*.

In 1891, Charles B. Hancock commissioned Christensen to paint a panorama detailing early periods of tension experienced by the Latter-day Saint communities.[28] Of the panorama's eight panels, four depict persecution in Missouri in the 1830s and Illinois in the 1840s. Another shows the Mormon Battalion in 1847. Three additional images relate to the Walker War (a series of raids, mostly in Sanpete County, between the settlers and the Utes led by Chief Walkara, in 1853).[29] Hancock, who served in the Mormon Battalion, was a colonel in the Utah territorial militia in the 1850s and witnessed many of the scenes in the panorama. The Hancock images, which recalled events of thirty to fifty years earlier, reveal not so much how things happened, but how Latter-day Saint settlers of the 1890s interpreted or even fantasized about history. Richard Jensen and Richard Oman point out the strong lighting in some scenes, noting that in one "a very consistent light source from the upper right is indicated, making the time about 2:00 p.m."[30] Christensen incorporated these kinds of details to draw attention to the fact that he is presenting the image as a true visual testimony of how things really happened. Whether the scene is accurate or not (and it is safe to say Christensen *is* taking a substantial amount of artistic license), Christensen is presenting it as truth.

In *Indian Fight at Salt Creek [Nephi], 1855* (Fig. 4.3) from the Hancock Panorama, two different events are combined into one image to tell a story.[31]

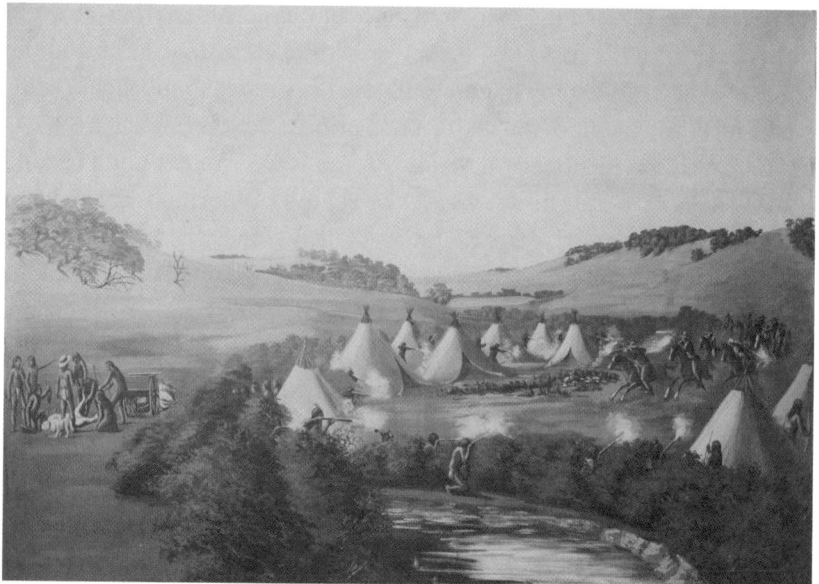

Figure 4.3 C. C. A. Christensen, *Indian Fight at Salt Creek, 1855*, c. 1891, Church History Library, The Church of Jesus Christ of Latter-day Saints.

The main image on the right depicts the fallout after failed negotiations between Hancock and a band of Timpanogos. The militia rides into the camp and is encircled by a volley of gunshots from Native men hiding behind teepees and bushes. Hancock, in his signature wide-brimmed hat, is caught between the shooting parties and lies on the ground injured. Not depicted are the several Timpanogos who were killed in the skirmish. The small scene on the left occurred two weeks later, when settler Ferney F. Tindrel was killed and scalped.[32] Christensen emphasizes the violence by showing Tindrel and his horse lying on the ground with their chests full of arrows. One Timpanogos proudly holds up the man's scalp, another wears his hat, and others strip him of his boots and clothing. Taken together, the two scenes project a story of white men trying, unsuccessfully, to coexist with ferocious Natives.

Christensen juxtaposed the Mormon settlers with the Indigenous people even more explicitly in a pair of paintings of the Manti Temple site. The first, *The Manti Temple* (Fig. 4.4), is a triumphalist view of the Mormon structure dominating the surrounding landscape. Carefully designed terraces lined with small trees are paired with zig-zagging staircases that pull

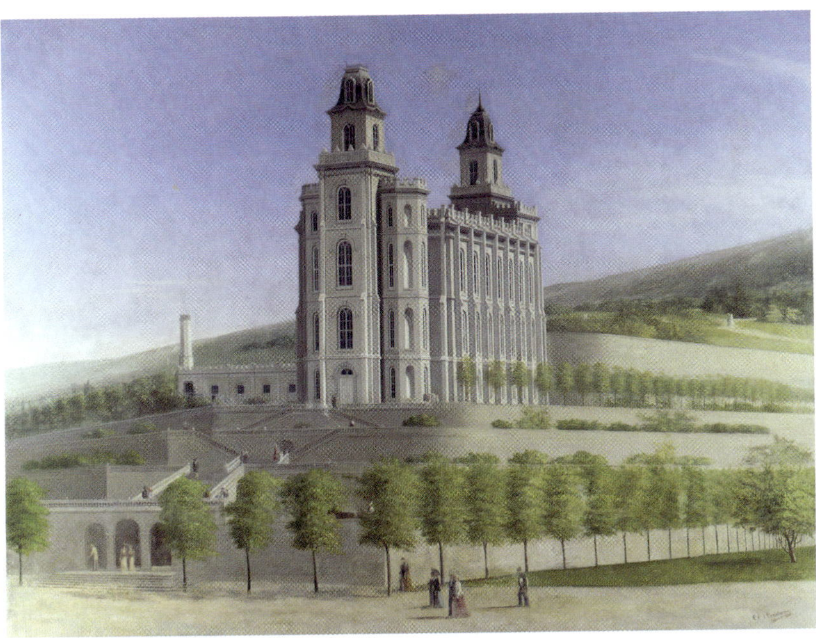

Figure 4.4 C. C. A. Christensen, *Rendering of the Manti Temple (The Manti Temple)*, c. 1889, oil on canvas, 54½ × 72⅜ inches, Church History Museum, The Church of Jesus Christ of Latter-day Saints.

the viewer's eye up toward the soaring temple towers. Small human figures walking below put the enormous man-made construction in perspective. The Sanpete Stake Relief Society commissioned the work for the 1893 World's Columbian Exposition, hoping to challenge existing stereotypes about the Latter-day Saints.[33] Christensen's detailed depiction of the temple, within a pristine western landscape peopled with well-dressed ladies and gentlemen, showcases the industry and refinement of the Sanpete settlers. In effect, it announces to Americans outside Utah, "We are just like you."

Shortly after, Christensen painted another view of the Manti Temple site, this time imagining how it looked before development. *Temple Hill in Manti, November 1849* (Fig. 4.5) was painted in 1893. It is the exact width of the *Manti Temple* canvas, but only half as tall. Together, the pair of images visualizes the narrative pushed by Latter-day Saints at the time that, as Reeve summarizes, "they were the agents of civilization, people who prevailed over the wilderness and its savage inhabitants to spread American ideals westward."[34] The foreground is filled with a quiet Ute encampment,

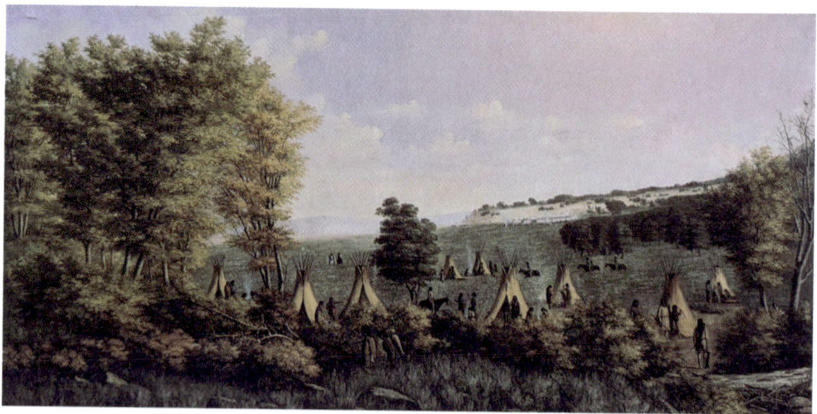

Figure 4.5 C. C. A. Christensen, *Temple Hill in Manti, November 1849 (Indian Encampment at Manti)*, 1893, oil on canvas, 36 × 72 inches, Church History Museum, The Church of Jesus Christ of Latter-day Saints.

including women and children, at the base of the hill. Barely visible in the distance is a circle of Conestoga wagons. Near the center of the canvas, two mounted scouts from the wagon party ride toward the Utes—this is the moment right before initial contact between the two nations. There is a visual echo of the ring of teepees in the circle of wagons, and campfire smoke rises from both groupings. These similarities between the Ute and settler camps heighten the effect when this scene is compared with *The Manti Temple*. The enormous progress made by the settlers is put in stark relief against the fate of the Utes, who started from the same humble circumstances in the same place but are now absent from the scene. This type of comparison is a pictorial device Christensen used in his earlier Huntington Panorama. There, too, he depicted the same geographical location repeatedly (in that case, the Hill Cumorah) to show the passage of time and visualize the restoration of the Gospel.

There are undertones of nostalgia and national pride in *Temple Hill in Manti*. By 1893 in Manti, Ute bands had been relegated to history. With no one left for settlers to fear or compete with, the portrayals of violence in the Hancock Panorama give way here for a more romantic imagining of peaceful Indigenous life before the settlers. Even the trees, while quite different from the orderly rows of settler-planted saplings in *The Manti Temple*, are given careful attention in a style reminiscent of Albert Bierstadt's sweeping Western landscapes. Still, though, in the Ute scene, the tiny people are small beneath the towering trees, whereas in the Temple scene, the miniature people are subsumed within man-made structures. The message is that the Latter-day Saints, as good Americans, helped expand the nation by imposing order and righteousness on a wild and pagan place.[35] Both original paintings are still displayed in the Manti Temple today.

These themes appear again in Christensen's most well-known work, *The Handcart Company* (Fig. 4.6) from 1900. A group of bedraggled but determined Latter-day Saint men, women, and children cross a stream on the American prairie. In a compositional reversal from the earlier *Temple Hill in Manti*, the pioneers are emphasized in the foreground while a few Indigenous riders gallop toward them from the distant background.[36] In the handcart grouping on the left, several people notice the approaching men and stop in their tracks. A few point to alert the others. Meanwhile, most of the exhausted pioneers are busy setting up camp, building fires, and nursing babies—unaware of the approaching threat. Christensen conveys the message that the Latter-day Saints, expelled from state after state in the Union, are on their own to protect themselves. Viewers in the year 1900, though, knew that the story ended in pioneer triumph. So, the Indigenous

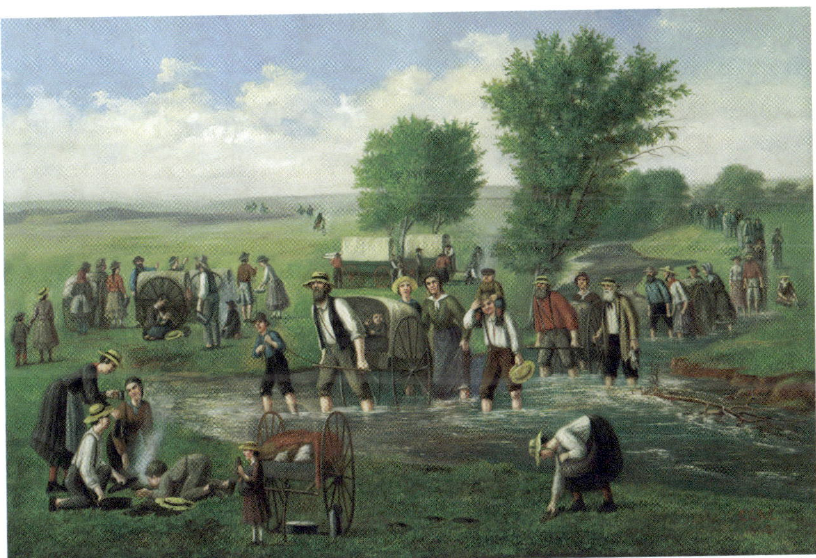

Figure 4.6 C. C. A. Christensen, *The Handcart Company (Handcart Pioneers)*, 1900, oil on canvas, 25⅜ × 38⁵⁄₁₆ inches, Church History Museum, The Church of Jesus Christ of Latter-day Saints.

riders provide a contrast to the pioneers, highlighting the latter's bravery, peacefulness, and civilized order. Visually, the contrast is heightened by the intersection of the pioneers' horizontal line of movement and the Native Americans' vertical line of approach. The painting makes heroes of courageous but common settlers seeking to build the New Jerusalem.

Scandinavian Heritage

As these pioneers (many of whom were European immigrants) came to Utah, Church leaders encouraged assimilation in language, culture, and belief. An 1886 editorial in the *Deseret News* praised Scandinavians as "a class of immigrants who strive to assimilate as rapidly as they can to Americans" and especially noted their ability "to acquire the language and customs of the country and become identified with its institutions."[37] In 1901, in response to attempts by a group of Utah Swedes to emphasize their Swedish heritage, the First Presidency issued an epistle declaring "The counsel of the Church to all Saints of foreign birth who come here is that they should learn to speak English as soon as possible, adopt the manners and customs of the American people, fit themselves to become good and loyal citizens of this country, and by their good works show that they are true and faithful Latter-day Saints."[38]

The fledgling Latter-day Saint communities were often successful at melding various cultural backgrounds, but geographic pockets of British, Danish, Norwegian, and other groups formed. Sanpete County became one of the areas to which Danish Saints gathered. Today, a sign at the entrance to Ephraim still declares it "Little Denmark." One area in which many Swedes settled was nearby Emery County, just over the Manti-La Sal mountain range.

Although they worked at assimilation, the Scandinavians also found ways to perpetuate their unique heritage and meld it with their new Latter-day Saint identity. In certain areas, Church meetings were offered in Danish or Swedish rather than English.[39] Some settlers observed traditional Scandinavian holidays, and the popular annual Scandinavian Celebration gathered enormous crowds.[40] The Danish newspaper in Utah, *Bikuben*, was published in the Danish language from 1876 until 1935. Swedish-language papers included *Svenska Härolden*, *Utah Korrespondenten*, and *Utah Posten*. Despite historical tensions between Denmark, Sweden, Norway, Finland, and Iceland, immigrants coming to Utah from these countries were typically lumped together as Scandinavians. We might think of Utah Danish Latter-day Saint identity at the turn of the century in several narrowing levels: first, Latter-day Saint; second, American; third, Scandinavian; and fourth, Danish.

At the dawn of the twentieth century, as Church leaders tried to highlight their Americanness, Christensen suddenly focused on his native Scandinavia. His writing and art of this time are marked by nostalgia for the old country. As an elderly man, he emphasized the goodness of his native land and people, seemingly forgetting his zealous youthful writings about the immorality and injustice of "Babylon." He was not alone in this, as other Utah Scandinavians at the time similarly looked fondly back at their heritage, preparing for a jubilee in June 1900 to commemorate fifty years since missionaries first preached in Copenhagen. As part of the festivities, Andrew Jenson, an Assistant Church Historian and a Danish immigrant, prepared a memorial book with photos, biographies, and a written history. Jenson's speech at the celebration recalled the early struggles of Scandinavians to be fully accepted by Church members and leaders, who were predominantly American and British.[41] By the turn of the century, Christensen, Jenson, and other Scandinavians seemed to feel more secure in their social status and potential for leadership roles within the Church. Yet, the decades of Scandinavian particularity in Utah—including insular communities, separate Church services, and Scandinavian-language newspapers, hymnbooks, scriptures, and pamphlets—left a lingering sense of distinctiveness.

In his later years, Christensen wrote extensively in Danish: poetry, hymns, editorials, letters, and histories. In his retrospective on Christensen, William Mulder wrote,

> Carl Christian Anton Christensen and his Danish verse were something of an institution among the Scandinavians in Utah and their fellow 'Mormoner' in 'de gamle Land,' the old country [Denmark, Norway, Sweden]. They sang his hymns from their little pocket *Salmer for de Sidst Doges Hellige*, heard his reunion pieces, and read his rhymed letters and humorous sketches as they appeared from time to time in *Bikuben* or *Skandinaviens Stjerne*.[42]

In one of Christensen's allegorical poems about the afterlife, he imagined a heavenly-organized Scandinavian Stake, in which Danes spoke only Danish.[43] In addition to producing his own Danish writing, Christensen taught Danish at the Sanpete Stake Academy from 1893–1899. As this allegiance to the Danish language indicates, Christensen never lost his connection to the country of his birth. He was especially concerned that the younger generation born in Utah should learn Danish and know their heritage. In 1910, he recited his poem "Old Affections Don't Wear Out" at the annual Scandinavian Celebration. The first lines read:

> Who can ever forget
> The dear sound of the mother tongue—
> Forget Mother's sweet voice,
> When she sang for her small ones?—
> Sang of Denmark's meadows and fields
> And her able men and youth—
> No! because memories of the home of childhood
> Bind me to its speech.[44]

As part of Christensen's efforts to preserve Scandinavian heritage and history, he asked his friend Anthon H. Lund (an apostle in the Church) for an appointment to work in the Church Historian's Office. Starting there in 1901, Christensen helped Andrew Jenson research and write *History of the Scandinavian Mission*. Jenson was slightly younger than Christensen but shared his zeal for recording and archiving the history of the Latter-day Saints. Jenson was committed to preserving in careful detail the experiences of the Scandinavian Latter-day Saints both in their native land and in America.[45] The final book was not published until 1927, fifteen years after Christensen's death, and it did not credit his work on it. Yet Christensen's wry style is evident, especially in chapters chronicling the early years of the mission when Christensen served there. For example, chapter 22 includes a story of Elders Carl C. A. Christensen and Carl C. N. Dorius narrowly escaping arrest for public preaching in Norway by cleverly pretending to be a Mormon and a Lutheran discussing the Bible.[46] In detail and phrasing, the recounting is nearly identical to Christensen's earlier telling of the story from a first-person perspective in his "Early Missionary Experiences" in the *Juvenile Instructor*.[47]

In the early 1900s, Christensen's focus on his birthplace also took the form of at least eight small landscape studies of Scandinavia that he executed from memory. For example, *Missionaries Preaching in Denmark* (Fig. 4.7) depicts a charming Danish farming town where two Latter-day Saint elders share the good news with a woman outside her house. As always, Christensen carefully attended to the details of landscape and common folk. Here, he included a low stone wall that ends in a wooden gate, a ladder propped against a house, a cow grazing, and a man passing by in a horse-drawn wagon that kicks up dust. Christensen painted this in 1903, during the time he worked with Jenson compiling a history of the Scandinavian mission. Christensen painted several such scenes in 1903 and 1904, which was years after his return to Utah from his Scandinavian mission and decades after his immigration to Utah. They visually echo his poems of the time, such as these lines from "Love Will Never Grow Old," sung at the festival in Ephraim in May 1901:

> The springtime of youth we remember
> With its blossoms and sunshiny days
> But old age, like the days of December
> Have few of Sun's beautiful rays.
> Yet the sun is still there
> And the blossoms that were
> We shall find on that beautiful shore;
> And the friends which we loved
> There will greet us
> And then they will leave us no more.[48]

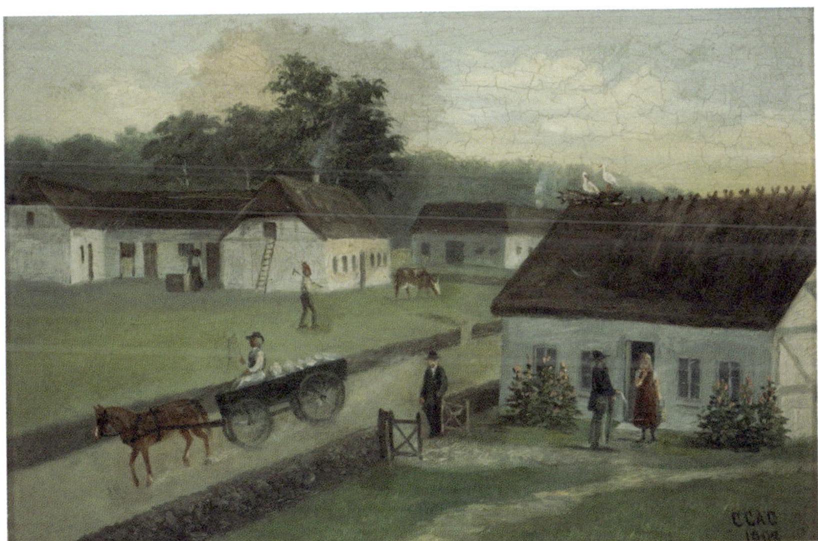

Figure 4.7 C. C. A. Christensen, *Missionaries Preaching in Denmark*, 1903, oil on canvas, 6½ × 9½ inches, estate of Louise Jackson Nuland. Image courtesy of the Church History Museum, The Church of Jesus Christ of Latter-day Saints.

Conclusions

Christensen's understanding of cultural heritage and identity paralleled the changing ways in which Latter-day Saints positioned themselves in relation to Americans. In the mid-to-late nineteenth century, Christensen depicted the injustice inflicted by Americans upon the Latter-day Saints. The Mormon Panorama, which he and his son showed throughout the Mormon West for years, helped disseminate this persecution narrative. He also showcased Latter-day Saint successes in the West, despite their exile from the United States. His poetry and art of this time are zealous and forward-looking.

During the last two decades of the twentieth century, the Saints were forced to reevaluate this insular narrative. United States expansion, technological advances, and political forces shifted the balance of power. The Latter-day Saints, in dealing with federal raids against polygamy and repeated denials of their request for Utah statehood, had to reposition themselves as good American citizens. One way they did this was to use Indigenous figures as a foil to American Latter-day Saints. Christensen's art reflects this shift in the way his images of Indigenous people changed dramatically from the 1870s to the 1890s.

Through it all, Christensen's Scandinavian heritage remained an important part of his identity. In the early twentieth century, with statehood secured and expectations of an impending apocalypse dwindling, Latter-day Saints were able to examine their past and plan for their future. In his final years, Christensen encouraged a particularly Scandinavian kind of Mormon identity in his writing and with his sentimental paintings of Scandinavian towns and landscapes. By its nature, this cultural heritage was exclusive but still located as a subset of Western Mormonism. There is sometimes a tension apparent in Christensen's work between involvement in both these larger and smaller communities—a cultural tension that continues today for members of the global Church. The body of work left by Christensen indicates that by the end of his life he saw room to meld these identities in a fruitful way.

Bibliographic Essay

The copious amount of artwork and writing produced by C. C. A. Christensen makes him an exceptional figure in the early history of The Church of Jesus Christ of Latter-day Saints. It is hard to think of any other Latter-day Saint visual artist, even today, who wrote as much as Christensen did. This body of work allows unique glimpses into the beliefs and life experiences of nineteenth-century members of the Church in Utah. While Christensen's early art and writing were informed by an eager millenarian spirit, his later work shifted to a focus on preserving the past and building a solid foundation for future generations.

Christensen's Artwork

Christensen painted more scenes, by far, of Church history and scripture than any other artist of the nineteenth century. Add to that his many genre scenes and landscapes of Utah and Scandinavia, and there are ninety-seven known Christensen paintings. Some of these appear to be preparatory sketches or reworkings of more finished works. A few are known from written descriptions but are no longer extant.[1]

Largest in size of the extant works are Christensen's twenty-two Mormon Panorama panels, which are in the collection of the Brigham Young University (BYU) Museum of Art. The first panel, now missing, depicted Joseph Smith's first vision of Heavenly Father and Jesus Christ. The remaining scenes are:

1. *The Hill Cumorah*, c. 1878, tempera on muslin, 78¼ × 114¼ inches, Brigham Young University Museum of Art, gift of the grandchildren of C. C. A. Christensen, 1970.

2. *Tarring and Feathering the Prophet*, c. 1878, tempera on muslin, 78¼ × 114¼ inches, Brigham Young University Museum of Art, gift of the grandchildren of C. C. A. Christensen, 1970.
3. *Saints Driven from Jackson County Missouri*, c. 1878, tempera on muslin, 78¼ × 114¼ inches, Brigham Young University Museum of Art, gift of the grandchildren of C. C. A. Christensen, 1970.
4. *Zion's Camp*, c. 1878, tempera on muslin, 77¼ × 113 inches, Brigham Young University Museum of Art, gift of the grandchildren of C. C. A. Christensen, 1970.
5. *Mobbers on the Missouri River*, c. 1878, tempera on muslin, 77¼ × 113 inches, Brigham Young University Museum of Art, gift of the grandchildren of C. C. A. Christensen, 1970.
6. *The Battle of Crooked River*, c. 1878, tempera on muslin, 77¼ × 113 inches, Brigham Young University Museum of Art, gift of the grandchildren of C. C. A. Christensen, 1970.
7. *Haun's Mill*, c. 1878, tempera on muslin, 77¼ × 113 inches, Brigham Young University Museum of Art, gift of the grandchildren of C. C. A. Christensen, 1970.
8. *The Arrest of Mormon Leaders*, c. 1878, tempera on muslin, 77¼ × 113 inches, Brigham Young University Museum of Art, gift of the grandchildren of C. C. A. Christensen, 1970.
9. *Liberty Jail*, c. 1878, tempera on muslin, 77¼ × 113 inches. Brigham Young University Museum of Art, gift of the grandchildren of C. C. A. Christensen, 1970.
10. *Leaving Missouri*, c. 1878, tempera on muslin, 77¼ × 113 inches, Brigham Young University Museum of Art, gift of the grandchildren of C. C. A. Christensen, 1970.
11. *Joseph Preaching to the Indians*, c. 1878, tempera on muslin, 77¼ × 113 inches, Brigham Young University Museum of Art, gift of the grandchildren of C. C. A. Christensen, 1970.
12. *Joseph Mustering the Nauvoo Legion*, c. 1878, tempera on muslin, 77¼ × 113 inches, Brigham Young University Museum of Art, gift of the grandchildren of C. C. A. Christensen, 1970.
13. *Interior of Carthage Jail*, c. 1878, tempera on muslin, 77¼ × 113 inches, Brigham Young University Museum of Art, gift of the grandchildren of C. C. A. Christensen, 1970.
14. *Exterior of Carthage Jail*, c. 1878, tempera on muslin, 77¼ × 113 inches, Brigham Young University Museum of Art, gift of the grandchildren of C. C. A. Christensen, 1970.

15. *The Nauvoo Temple*, c. 1878, tempera on muslin, 77¼ × 113 inches, Brigham Young University Museum of Art, gift of the grandchildren of C. C. A. Christensen, 1970.
16. *Burning of the Temple*, c. 1878, tempera on muslin, 77¼ × 113 inches, Brigham Young University Museum of Art, gift of the grandchildren of C. C. A. Christensen, 1970.
17. *Crossing the Mississippi on the Ice*, c. 1878, tempera on muslin, 77¼ × 113 inches, Brigham Young University Museum of Art, gift of the grandchildren of C. C. A. Christensen, 1970.
18. *The Battle of Nauvoo*, c. 1878, tempera on muslin, 77¼ × 113 inches, Brigham Young University Museum of Art, gift of the grandchildren of C. C. A. Christensen, 1970.
19. *Catching Quails*, c. 1878, tempera on muslin, 77¼ × 113 inches, Brigham Young University Museum of Art, gift of the grandchildren of C. C. A. Christensen, 1970.
20. *Winter Quarters*, c. 1878, tempera on muslin, 77¼ × 113 inches, Brigham Young University Museum of Art, gift of the grandchildren of C. C. A. Christensen, 1970.
21. *Pioneers Crossing the Plains of Nebraska*, c. 1878, tempera on muslin, 77¼ × 113 inches, Brigham Young University Museum of Art, gift of the grandchildren of C. C. A. Christensen, 1970.
22. *Entering the Great Salt Lake Valley*, c. 1878, tempera on muslin, 77¼ × 113 inches, Brigham Young University Museum of Art, gift of the grandchildren of C. C. A. Christensen, 1970.

The Church History Museum preserves Christensen's painted series on the life of Nephi; the Huntington Panorama scroll; the surviving images of the Hancock Panorama; a photograph of a painting of Christ in America (current location of the original painting is unknown); the iconic *The Handcart Company*; two views of the Manti Temple site; two lithographs; a small landscape; and drawings and paintings in his journals.

1. *Lehi Preaching to the Jews (Life of Nephi series for Deseret Sunday School Union)*, c. 1890, oil on composition board, 24¾ × 18⅝ inches, Church History Museum.
2. *Departure of Lehi and His Family from Jerusalem (Life of Nephi series for Deseret Sunday School Union)*, c. 1890, oil on composition board, 24¾ × 18⅝ inches, Church History Museum.
3. *Nephi and Zoram with the Brass Plates (Life of Nephi series for Deseret Sunday School Union)*, c. 1890, oil on composition board, 24¾ × 18⅝ inches, Church History Museum.

4. *Nephi's Vision of the Virgin and Child (Life of Nephi series for Deseret Sunday School Union)*, c. 1890, oil on composition board, 24¾ × 18⅝ inches, Church History Museum.
5. *The Finding of the Compass [Liahona] (Life of Nephi series for Deseret Sunday School Union)*, c. 1890, oil on composition board, 24¾ × 18⅝ inches, Church History Museum.
6. *The Building of the Ship (Life of Nephi series for Deseret Sunday School Union)*, c. 1890, oil on composition board, 24¾ × 18⅝ inches, Church History Museum.
7. *Nephi Making the Plates for the Records (Life of Nephi series for Deseret Sunday School Union)*, c. 1890, oil on composition board, 24¾ × 18⅝ inches, Church History Museum.
8. *Lehi Blessing His Posterity (Life of Nephi series for Deseret Sunday School Union)*, c. 1890, oil on composition board, 24¾ × 18⅝ inches, Church History Museum.
9. *The Separation of the Nephites and Lamanites (Life of Nephi series for Deseret Sunday School Union)*, c. 1890, oil on composition board, 24¾ × 18⅝ inches, Church History Museum.
10. *The Building of the Temple (Life of Nephi series for Deseret Sunday School Union)*, c. 1890, oil on composition board, 24¾ × 18⅝ inches, Church History Museum.
11. Photograph of *Mobbers Raiding Printing Property & Store at Independence, Mo., July 20, 1883 (Hancock Panorama)*, c. 1891, Church History Museum.
12. Photograph of *Hancock & Company's Exit from Jackson Co. Mo. Nov. 1833 (Hancock Panorama)*, c. 1891, Church History Museum.
13. Photograph of *Carthage Jail, Hancock Co., Ill. June 27, 1844 (Hancock Panorama)*, c. 1891, Church History Museum.
14. Photograph of *Attack by Mobbers on the Hancock Homestead. Hancock Co. Ill. (Hancock Panorama)*, c. 1891, Church History Museum.
15. Photograph of *Morman [Mormon] Battalion Celebrating 4 July 1847. Los Angelos [Los Angeles], Cal. (Hancock Panorama)*, c. 1891, Church History Museum.
16. Photograph of *Utah Chiefs War Council, July 16, 1853, Payson, Utah (Hancock Panorama)*, c. 1891, Church History Museum.
17. Photograph of *Indian Fight at Salt Creek, 1855 (Hancock Panorama)*, c. 1891, Church History Museum.
18. Photograph of *Indian Reserve Scene of Agency of Peete Teetneets Band, 1857, Utah Co. (Hancock Panorama)*, c. 1891, Church History Museum.

19. *Adam and Eve in the Garden (Untitled [Huntington/Lamanite Panorama])*, c. 1871–1875, oil on linen, 26 × 24 inches, Church History Museum.
20. *Cain and Abel (Untitled [Huntington/Lamanite Panorama])*, c. 1871–1875, oil on linen, 26 × 24 inches, Church History Museum.
21. *Noah and the Ark (Untitled [Huntington/Lamanite Panorama])*, c. 1871–1875, oil on linen, 26 × 24 inches, Church History Museum.
22. *Lehi's Family Leaving Jerusalem (Untitled [Huntington/Lamanite Panorama])*, c. 1871–1875, oil on linen, 26 × 24 inches, Church History Museum.
23. *Nephi Tied to the Mast (Untitled [Huntington/Lamanite Panorama])*, c. 1871–1875, oil on linen, 26 × 24 inches, Church History Museum.
24. *Lehi's Family Arriving in the Promised Land (Untitled [Huntington/Lamanite Panorama])*, c. 1871–1875, oil on linen, 26 × 24 inches, Church History Museum.
25. *Baptism of Jesus with the Holy Ghost in the Form of Dove (Untitled [Huntington/Lamanite Panorama])*, c. 1871–1875, oil on linen, 26 × 24 inches, Church History Museum.
26. *Crucifixion of Christ (Untitled [Huntington/Lamanite Panorama])*, c. 1871–1875, oil on linen, 26 × 24 inches, Church History Museum.
27. *Christ and His Disciples in the New World (Untitled [Huntington/Lamanite Panorama])*, c. 1871–1875, oil on linen, 26 × 24 inches, Church History Museum.
28. *Moroni Hiding the Plates (Untitled [Huntington/Lamanite Panorama])*, c. 1871–1875, oil on linen, 26 × 24 inches, Church History Museum.
29. *Moroni Giving the Plates to Joseph Smith (Untitled [Huntington/Lamanite Panorama])*, c. 1871–1875, oil on linen, 26 × 24 inches, Church History Museum.
30. Photograph of *Christ in the New World*, 1903, Church History Museum.
31. *The Handcart Company (Handcart Pioneers)*, 1900, oil on canvas, 25⅜ × 38 5⁄16 inches, Church History Museum.
32. *Rendering of the Manti Temple (The Manti Temple)*, c. 1889, oil on canvas, 54½ × 72⅜ inches, Church History Museum.
33. *Temple Hill in Manti, November 1849 (Indian Encampment at Manti)*, c. 1893, oil on canvas, 36 × 72 inches, Church History Museum.
34. *The Angel Moroni Delivering the Plates of the Book of Mormon to Joseph Smith Jun.*, 1886, lithograph, 19 × 12⅝ inches, printed by F. E. Bording, Copenhagen, Church History Museum.
35. *The Restoration of the Aaronic Priesthood. Joseph Smith Jun. and Oliver Cowdery Being Ordained by the Angel, John the Baptist, May 15, 1829*,

1887, lithograph, 18 × 14 inches, printed by F. E. Bording, Copenhagen, Church History Museum.

36. *Rural Scene in Salt Lake Valley*, 1902, oil on board, 7¼ × 14⅝ inches, Church History Museum.
37. *B. Y. Calling Volunteers for the Mormon-Battalion*, no date, oil on canvas, 13½ × 22$^{5}/_{16}$ inches, Church History Museum.
38. *View of Utah Lake from the West Side, Mt. Nebo in the Background*, c. 1865, watercolor on paper, 3½ × 5½ inches, in C. C. A. Christensen Diary, 26 April–23 July 1865, Church History Museum.

The Springville Museum of Art houses *Weighing the Baby, Winter Quarters*, and *Handcart Pioneers' First View of the Salt Lake Valley. Immigration of the Saints* is in the collection of the Daughters of the Utah Pioneers. The Utah Museum of Fine Arts has *Home! Sweet Home!* Christensen's mural in the Manti Temple remains in the endowment room there.

1. *Weighing the Baby*, 1872, oil on canvas, 8 × 10 inches, Springville Museum of Art, gift from Diane and Sam Stewart, Salt Lake City.
2. *Winter Quarters*, 1891, oil on canvas, 14 × 22 inches, Springville Museum of Art, gift from A. Merlin and Alice Steed trust.
3. *Handcart Pioneers' First View of the Salt Lake Valley*, 1890, oil on canvas, 16 × 12 inches, Springville Museum of Art, gift from Neil and Jane Schaerrer, Salt Lake City.
4. *Immigration of the Saints*, 1878, oil on canvas, 34⅛ × 50 inches, Daughters of the Utah Pioneers Museum.
5. *Home! Sweet Home!*, 1875, oil on panel, 12¼ × 18½ inches, Utah Museum of Fine Arts, gift of Mr. and Mrs. Joseph J. Palmer.
6. *Creation Room Mural*, c. 1886–1887, oil on gesso, 16 feet high, Manti Temple, © by Intellectual Reserve, Inc.

Many of Christensen's other paintings of Church history or of landscapes are in private collections, often passed down through his descendants. With some updates, the details and provenance for most of the works below are from the 1984 catalog by Richard L. Jensen and Richard G. Oman, *C. C. A. Christensen, 1831–1912: Mormon Immigrant Artist*.

1. *Portrait of Eliza and Charles John Christensen*, c. 1864, oil on canvas, private collection, estate of Mrs. Geniel H. Jensen.
2. *Emigrant Ship*, 1867, watercolor and ink on paper, 7 × 10¾ inches, private collection, estate of Erla Coulston.

3. *Home of J. F. F. Dorius in Ephraim*, 1876, oil on canvas, 11 13/16 × 16 inches, private collection, estate of Mrs. Geniel H. Jensen.
4. *John the Baptist Ordaining Joseph Smith and Oliver Cowdery*, c. 1886, oil on paper, 12¾ × 9½ inches, private collection of Rosalie K. Guerin.
5. *Sugar Creek*, 1885, oil on canvas, 14⅛ × 22⅛ inches, Norma Taggart estate.
6. *Defense of Nauvoo in September 1846*, 1886, oil on canvas, 13⅞ × 22 inches, private collection, estate of Mrs. Edith Joy Cannon.
7. *Liberty Jail Clay Co., Mo.*, no date, oil on canvas, 12 × 17 inches, private collection, estate of Mr. and Mrs. Neil D. Schaerrer.
8. *Crossing the Mississippi Feb: 1846*, no date, oil on canvas, 13¾ × 22½ inches, private collection, estate of Mr. and Mrs. Morgan Dyreng.
9. *Mormon Battallion Ball, July 1846*, no date, oil on canvas, 13 7/16 × 22⅜ inches, private collection.
10. *Crossing the Missouri River*, no date, oil on canvas, 13 3/16 × 22⅝ inches, private collection, estate of Mrs. Earl Dorius.
11. *Winter Quarters 1846–1847*, no date, oil on canvas, 13 15/16 × 22 inches, Norma Taggart estate.
12. *Pioneers Crossing the North Platte near Chimney Rock*, no date, oil on paper, 8 1/16 × 10 inches, private collection of Mr. and Mrs. Vernon Jensen.
13. *View of the Salt Lake Valley*, no date, oil on broadcloth, 8⅞ × 16¼ inches, private collection of Mr. and Mrs. Vernon Jensen.
14. *Wagon Train Entering the Valley of the Great Salt Lake*, no date, oil on canvas, 7⅞ × 11 1/16 inches, private collection of Mr. and Mrs. Vernon Jensen.
15. *Skaters*, 1891, oil on board, 12 3/16 × 18 3/16 inches, private collection of Beatrice Vernon.
16. *Pioneers and Indians at a River Crossing*, c. 1879, oil on paper, 11 13/16 × 15⅞ inches, private collection of Mr. and Mrs. Vernon Jensen.
17. *Summer in the Mountains of Norway*, 1891, oil on board, 12⅜ × 18½ inches, private collection of Julia Astle.
18. *Missionaries Preaching in Denmark*, 1903, oil on canvas, 6½ × 9½ inches, estate of Louise Jackson Nuland.
19. *Lake Scene*, 1903, oil on board, 8½ × 18 inches, private collection of James Harrison.
20. *Norwegian Fjord Scene*, oil on board, 9½ × 13 inches, private collection of Ruby Smith.
21. *Norwegian Village Scene*, 1903, oil on canvas, 6⅝ × 9½ inches, private collection, estate of Mrs. Veda Jensen.

22. *Cross-country Skier*, 1903, oil on canvas, 8¼ × 10 inches, private collection of Christine Gedig Ré.
23. *Handcart Pioneers*, 1903, oil on canvas, 11 × 15 inches, private collection of Joanne Bach.
24. *Handcart Pioneers Coming through the Mountains*, no date, oil on canvas, 15 × 24¹⁄₁₆ inches, private collection of Mrs. Mary Christensen Condie.
25. *Scene from Fjord on Norway's West Coast*, 1904, oil on canvas, 12 × 18 inches, private collection of Lans Christensen.
26. *Norway in Winter*, 1904, oil on canvas, 11¹⁄₁₆ × 15 inches, private collection of Donald and Sidney Wallace.
27. *Wheat Harvest in Ephraim*, no date, oil on paper, 9½ × 13 inches, private collection of Mr. Harry Sundwall.
28. *Harvest Time in Ephraim*, 1904, oil on canvas, 12 × 18 inches, private collection of Mr. J. William Christensen.
29. *Picking Flowers*, no date, oil on canvas, 5½ × 9 inches, private collection of Mrs. Rea Werntz.

Uses of Christensen's Artwork

Church leaders supported Christensen's artistic endeavors during his lifetime. Brigham Young invited him to paint the newly built Salt Lake theater in 1863. Christensen and Danquart Weggeland painted rooms in the St. George Temple in 1881. Then the Church hired the pair to paint murals in the Manti temple in 1887. Christensen was commissioned by his local Sanpete Stake Relief Society in 1889 to paint a large rendition of the Manti Temple. In 1890, the Deseret Sunday School Union, led by George Reynolds, chose ten of Christensen's paintings for an illustrated series on the life of Nephi. These paintings were made into lithographs by another artist, which were distributed to Sunday School teachers in the Mountain West and serialized in the *Juvenile Instructor*. Throughout these years, Church authorities endorsed Christensen's Mormon Panorama presentations.[2]

Today, a handful of Christensen's artworks appear in Church media, but not typically in the most widely viewed sources. For instance, the Church's Gospel Art resource page includes Christensen's *The Handcart Company (Handcart Pioneers)*, *Crossing the Mississippi on the Ice*, and *Winter Quarters*.[3] A few of these images appeared in manuals that are no longer in use. Only two Christensen images show up in the 2025 *Come, Follow Me* manuals on Church history: *Saints Driven from Jackson County Missouri*, and *Zion's Camp*.[4] Two online exhibitions available on the Church website contain select scenes from Christensen's 1890 Nephi series: "The Journey of Lehi's Family" and "From Plates to Pages: Writing and Reading the Book of Mormon."[5] Finally, the Church's Museum Store Art Catalog sells prints of Christensen's *The Manti Temple* and *The Handcart Company (Handcart Pioneers)*.[6] None of Christensen's Book of Mormon paintings are included in recent Church publications.

Christensen's Writings

In addition to his visual arts output, Christensen was a devoted writer. Beginning with his first mission diary, Christensen carefully recorded names, events, and travels throughout his life. He also wrote about spiritual experiences and doctrinal insights. He composed poems, silly songs, and hymns. Furthermore, during his travels for missionary or artistic work, he regularly wrote letters to his wife Elise, which are now in the Church History Library.[7] Many of Elise's letters back to C. C. A. are also in the Church History Library.[8]

Christensen wrote extensively for Latter-day Saint publications, primarily *Bikuben*. These essays, remembrances, poems, and letters afford a glimpse into the concerns of the times and Christensen's role in developing Latter-day Saint thought. A final source for Christensen's writing is the Mormon Panorama script, of which there are several versions.[9]

From a young age, Christensen seemed to have a penchant for crafting poetry and recording in prose the details of his life experiences and the environment around him. At age nineteen, he began his first journal with a "life sketch" up until that point in 1853. Over the years, he filled the pages of many journals or *dagboks*. The originals are now preserved in the Church History Library.[10] Many of the earlier journals written in Danish were translated into English by Orson B. West at the Church History Library and by Eva M. Gregersen, a certified genealogist. Christensen sometimes re-wrote his hastily penned daily entries later into new books with elegant cursive and minor edits or additions.[11] Similarly, his undated "C. C. A. Christensen reminiscences" was written by hand in English later in his life and sometimes draws directly from earlier journals.[12] Christensen clearly desired to preserve his story along with the history of the Latter-day Saints.

Apart from his more private writings, Christensen composed numerous articles, op-eds, and poems for newspapers. One of his most fully developed essays focused on fine art and detailed his views on arts education, artistic taste as a mirror of spiritual progression, and the economic role of art. The lengthy treatise, written in Danish and titled "The Fine Arts," was published by *Bikuben* in four parts between February and March 1892.[13] In this discourse, Christensen took a democratic approach to fine art, including everything from painting and quilts to woven rugs and cast-iron stoves. He saw in the artistry of everyday objects the ability to "make life pleasant and . . . ennoble the minds of both young and old."[14] He believed that the beauty found in nature testified that God is not only a skilled artist but also an "astronomer, geologist, mineralogist, botanist, physiologist, physician, lawgiver, and architect."[15] Furthermore, he believed men and women were taught the arts and sciences in the premortal life, and once on earth, could relearn those skills through inspiration from the Spirit of God.[16] Christensen urged his fellow Utahns to not only appreciate art but also to provide arts education for youth in schools.

Christensen saw an inevitable progression in all human cultures, from primitive living conditions to a more refined situation that included artistry. More than just an increase in temporal comforts, Christensen believed this change in artistic taste related directly to spiritual progression. He wrote that when civilization embraced the arts, it brought people "closer to the goal which God has set for mankind to aspire to in this life, with the promised opportunity for further progression in the life to come."[17] Echoing popular contemporary theories of the stages of civilization,[18] Christensen reflected on mankind's advancement from "the barbarism of ancient time to the exalted status of present society."[19] Always duty-bound, Christensen emphasized the moral imperative to use time wisely, continually striving for greater progress, learning, and understanding. Extrapolating from this essay and from his op-eds bemoaning what he considered the sad state of local architecture and city planning, it seems that Christensen believed achievements in the arts (broadly defined) directly reflected a culture's spiritual and moral progress.

Finally, in "The Fine Arts," Christensen turned his attention to the economic benefits of artistic production. Indeed, he believed that all trade, including factories, merchants, shipping companies, and railroads, owed their existence at some level to the art industry.[20] He argued that Utah might follow the example of the British economy, which he claimed grew from the export of fabrics and arts rather than from agriculture. Christensen worried about a scarcity of good-quality farmland in the Latter-day Saint settlements in Utah, especially as the population surged in the late nineteenth century. The solution he proposed was to institute a more robust arts education in Utah schools, which would lead to the younger generation building up entrepreneurial export businesses based on good design principles.[21]

While "The Fine Arts" was a call to action aimed at future generations of Latter-day Saints, Christensen also painstakingly recorded his people's past. First, over a period of eight months and in ten installments, he published "Early Missionary Experiences" in *Juvenile Instructor*.[22] This essay sketched the details of his conversion in 1850 and experiences of his first mission from 1853 to 1857. The recurring themes are denial of religious liberty by Norwegian authorities (including the imposition of fines and imprisonment), the discomforts and financial difficulties that he and his companions suffered (such as scant food, treks across muddy terrain, and passages on the chilly decks of steamships), and the ability of the missionaries to proclaim the Gospel and confound their opponents. Christensen recounted many debates with local police or citizens in which he was able to persuade others to his cause by some combination of God's grace and his own kindness, honesty, wit, knowledge, and understanding of both Latter-day Saint and Lutheran doctrine. Several times in "Early Missionary Experiences," Christensen joyfully compared himself and his companions to Paul and the apostles and martyrs of old. Of one lengthy prison stay, he wrote, "To this day the three weeks that I spent in that cell, together with my now deceased friend, the late Bishop C. Dorius, seem to be among the happiest and brightest days of my life."[23]

Christensen continued to look back to earlier years in a series of articles from 1894 to 1910 that chronicled his handcart journey to the Salt Lake Valley.[24] These writings are lively and humorous and provide one of the most detailed accounts of this unique pioneer experience. Christensen remembered that each person in the handcart company was only allowed fifteen pounds of goods. For him, this requirement meant the sorrowful surrender of his beloved collection of Danish books, a loss he mentioned several times in his memoirs. He discussed the trials of heat, rain, bad roads, hard work, a new diet, and a frustrating Scottish company captain who did not understand Danish customs or language. Ever the artist and poet, Christensen offered many vivid vignettes in these articles: a blind woman testing water depth at a river crossing, a girl with a wooden leg walking the plains, families staying up until midnight to cook bread in a shared Dutch oven, everyone collecting buffalo chips for fuel, the young children walking out ahead of the wagons to avoid the dust, men taking turns standing duty at night, and the immigrants' dusty sunburned faces and ragged clothing (except for the wooden Scandinavian shoes which he proudly remarked held up quite well).[25] Christensen would draw on these remembrances for his painting *The Handcart Company (Handcart Pioneers)*, which remains his best-known work today.

In a comparable way, Christensen's scripted lecture that accompanied presentations of the Mormon Panorama drew from firsthand accounts to enhance the striking visuals. Christensen consulted eyewitnesses, published accounts, photographs, and other artistic renderings of buildings and events in composing his own recounting of the historical moments depicted.[26] The lecture script even pointed out names of people in the scenes. With this specificity, the script heightened the feeling of objective historical accuracy implicit in the Mormon Panorama. As several versions of the lecture script remain, it is unfortunately difficult to know Christensen's exact original wording. Contemporary sources indicate that Christensen did deliver an address along with the art presentation, but sometimes, and especially in the later years, his son Charles John was the one to give the lecture. Moreover, one direct descendant was told by family that C. C. A. and Charles read from different versions of the script depending on their audience.[27]

A theme of injustice and religious persecution of the Latter-day Saints runs through all versions of the Mormon Panorama lecture script. This parallels the way the images dramatically visualize violence toward the Saints. For instance, in the scene of Haun's Mill, Christensen painted women and children frantically fleeing from armed militiamen as men and boys try desperately to defend themselves. To drive home the brutality of the moment, the lecture script describes the man beside the wagon as, "Father McBride, an aged veteran who had fought in the Revolutionary War to establish the freedom which he as an American citizen was entitled to enjoy, that of worshiping [*sic*] God according to the dictates of his own conscience. After being shot down with his own gun and yet on his bended knees pleading for mercy he was litterally [*sic*] cut to peaces [*sic*] with an old fashioned corn cutter."[28] For Christensen, it was not just that innocent civilians were targeted for their religious beliefs, but that it was sometimes the very citizens who had fought to establish religious liberty in the United States who suffered persecution and death. Scholar John Marsh commented on the poignancy of the scenes, writing, "Perhaps Christensen was unaware of the parallel but the scenes he chose embraced the passions of the melodramas of the day, for there were moments of intense personal revelation and great fortitude in the face of adversity, of commitment to an ideal and of the valiant defense of that ideal. Scenes of persecution and flight, of imprisonment and martyrdom succeeded one another."[29]

Christensen's commitment to his religious faith and his belief in religious freedom is evident throughout all his writings, from his diaries and letters to his formal essays and panorama script. He wanted to document for posterity, in both picture and word, the abuses suffered by the Latter-day Saints. Perhaps he felt discouraged that, as an older man living in the Sanpete community he had helped build, he continued to face arrest and criminal charges for his beliefs just as he had as an eager young missionary in Norway forty years earlier. On the other hand, he documented the triumph of the Saints in several essays describing his handcart experiences and in paintings such as *The Handcart Company (Handcart Pioneers)*. Christensen's art and writing never shied away from the challenges of living one's faith and did not hesitate to celebrate the efforts of Church members and what he saw as their providential protection.

Critical Reception and Legacy

Over the past 150 years, Christensen's popularity has ebbed and flowed. Christensen's contemporaries recognized his contributions to the Church but largely focused on his writing rather than his visual art. After 1921, little scholarly research examined Christensen's work, but his family preserved much of his art. Showings of some of this art in the 1970s revived interest in Christensen, mostly with an eye toward a nostalgic viewing of history and American folk art. Riding this wave of interest, curators at the Museum of Church History and Art in the early 1980s compiled a comprehensive survey of Christensen's life and work.[30] In the past decade, a few scholars reframed Christensen's contributions within larger discussions of Mormon history and memory making.

During his lifetime, colleagues lauded Christensen's contributions to the Church and especially to his Sanpete community. In 1906, Church President Joseph F. Smith wrote to him, "I have always admired your integrity to the great cause of truth and human redemption."[31] One year before his death, *Bikuben* published a special tribute to Christensen. It noted, "Among the many able men who have fought so courageously for the cause of truth and have planted the gospel's pearl of great price in the hearts of truth seekers, as well in speech as in writing, Patriarch C. C. A. Christensen stands in the first row."[32] Announcing his death in 1912, *Bikuben* ran a front-page story calling Christensen, "One of the Church's Great Ones."[33] The papers in Sanpete and other parts of Utah covered his accomplishments in art, writing, and Church service. One example of the many complimentary accounts of his work is found in Manti's *The Home Sentinel*:

> C. C. A. Christensen, the indefatigable Ephraim artist and painter, is now finishing a picture which will doubtless add fresh lustre [*sic*] to his already well-established reputation. The picture in question represents the Angel Moroni delivering the plates to the Prophet Joseph Smith, at the Hill Commorah [*sic*], Sep. 22nd, 1827; and so far as our idea of the event and scene is concerned, we think that Mr. Christensen's conception of the matter is a very good one. The work is undoubtedly the result of careful study and research.[34]

Additionally, newspapers throughout Utah described Christensen's presentations of the Mormon Panorama. In 1883, the *Deseret News* reported,

> A goodly number of people witnessed Brother C. C. A. Christensen's first exhibition of his improved 'Mormon Panorama' in the 13th Ward Assembly Room last night. The subjects treated upon are in themselves very instructive and interesting, as they portray some of the most important scenes of Church History, and necessarily work upon the tender feelings of an intelligent audience . . . Everybody, young and old, ought to go and see the 'Mormon Panorama.'[35]

Two years later and 150 miles north, *The Ogden Herald* recounted Christensen's presentation of the Mormon Panorama in the Fourth Ward schoolhouse. The article noted,

> The exhibition was a good one, not only for its merits as such, but for the vast amount of information on the history of the Church which is given . . . The most trying scenes which our people have passed through

> are vividly pictured, and we know of no better way of impressing these things upon the minds of the young than by a pictorial representation such as that which is now being exhibited through the country by Brother Christensen.[36]

In 1921, nine years after Christensen's passing, John S. Hansen published a memorial volume in Danish dedicated to Christensen. It included a biography and compilation of poetry and other writing, specifically fifty-five "religious poems, hymns and songs," seven "evangelical articles and theses," twenty-six "occasional poems," and thirteen "humorous" writings. In the preface, Hansen described Christensen as "an indefatigable and self-sacrificing laborer in the Lord's vineyard."[37] The book centers Christensen's writing rather than his painting. A 1947 article by William Mulder also focused on Christensen's poetry.[38] Indeed, although newspapers reported on his artistic endeavors, Christensen's fame seems to have stemmed primarily from literary pursuits. Even Christensen's gravestone in the Ephraim Park Cemetery depicts a book of poetry but contains no mention of painting.

After Hansen's volume, Christensen received little public attention. His family, however, helped to preserve his artwork. One grandson, Seymour Christensen, kept the Mormon Panorama in his Ephraim home before giving it to BYU in 1953. Historian Carl Carmer became aware of it and used the scenes to illustrate his essay on Latter-day Saint history in *American Heritage* in 1963.[39]

Then, in the 1970s, amid growing interest in American folk-art traditions, Christensen garnered more attention. Carmer re-ignited public fascination with Christensen when he published a lengthy article on the Mormon Panorama in *Art in America* in 1970. Carmer provided some biographical information on Christensen and a brief critique of the art, saying only, "The bright, clear colors, the vitality of the human figures, the strength of the compositions, give them a unique quality."[40] The article includes images of the panorama's surviving twenty-two scenes, but the paragraphs below each one focus on the history recounted rather than discussing the art itself.

Sparked by Carmer's article, the "re-discovery" of Christensen's art grew quickly. That same year, the Whitney Museum of American Art in New York hosted an exhibition of the Mormon Panorama.[41] In preparation for the exhibition, BYU staff and a few invited descendants removed Elise's careful stitching of the canvases from almost one hundred years earlier so the canvases could be framed and displayed individually.[42] Upon their return to Utah, the paintings were displayed at the Harris Fine Arts Center on the BYU campus. In 1978, art historian Jane Dillenberger focused much of her essay, "Mormonism and American Religious Art," on Christensen's paintings.[43]

When the Museum of Church History and Art opened in Salt Lake City in 1984, its inaugural exhibition was a retrospective on Christensen. The accompanying catalog by Richard Jensen and Richard Oman contained the first methodical (and still the most comprehensive) compilation of Christensen's art.[44] Jensen and Oman did careful research into Christensen's life in Utah and Denmark, translated many of Christensen's journals and writings, interviewed his descendants, and conducted art historical research on the paintings.

Christensen's visibility diminished over the next two decades, but in the early twentieth century, BYU Museum of Art curator Paul Anderson helped to renew interest in Christensen's work. In 2003, the museum exhibited the panels of the Mormon Panorama.[45] Richard Jensen and Dawn Pheysey, the museum's curator of religious art, lectured on Christensen's life and the history of the panorama format. The museum hosted reenactments of Christensen's Mormon Panorama presentation, including a reading of the script, piano accompaniment, and hymn singing.[46] In 2005, Anderson continued these reenactments at This Is the Place Heritage Park in Salt Lake City. With a large replica of the scroll, Anderson assumed the character of C. C. A. Christensen and delivered his lecture from the script (Danish accent and all).[47]

Recently, a handful of scholars have probed deeper into Christensen's life and art. Noel Carmack, associate professor at Utah State University Eastern, considered Christensen's Book of Mormon paintings and panoramas in several articles.[48] Scholars Laura Hurtado and David Grua published a short essay examining one panel of the Mormon Panorama in 2013.[49] BYU Museum of Art religious art curator Ashlee Whitaker Evans organized a popular exhibition of the Mormon Panorama in 2015.[50] *Pioneer*, a publication of the National Society of the Sons of Utah Pioneers, printed images of the Huntington Panorama in 2019, alongside commentary by Hurtado.[51] Devan Jensen, executive editor at the BYU Religious Studies Center, also contributed to the *Pioneer* issue and conducted research on the Hancock Panorama.[52] In his book on Mormon memory making, BYU professor Steven Harper discussed how late-nineteenth-century presentations of the Mormon Panorama "catalyzed memory recursion."[53] BYU professor Julie Allen considered Christensen's combination of Danish art style and Mormon subject matter in a 2020 book chapter.[54] Nathan Rees, associate professor at the University of West Georgia, published a 2021 study of nineteenth-century Latter-day Saint art, highlighting the work of Christensen.[55] BYU professor James Swensen compared the legacies of Christensen and Carl Bloch in a 2023 article.[56] In 2024, BYU professor Heather Belnap focused on Christensen as one of five representative artists of the "Mormon-LDS Art Tradition" in an edited volume.[57] Also in 2024, scholars Evans, Rees, W. Paul Reeve, Terryl Givens, and Carlyle Constantino each considered artworks by Christensen in their essays in an edited volume on Latter-day Saint art.[58]

While interest in Christensen is on the rise, we might expect a greater volume of scholarly analysis of such an early and foundational writer and artist in the Latter-day Saint tradition. Yet, Christensen is not alone in this. There are few academic studies of most nineteenth-century Latter-day Saint artists. Recovering this legacy of early Latter-day Saint visual culture and writing provides a richer understanding of Church history and Mormon thought.

Notes

Chapter One. Journey of a Visionary

1. "'Mormon' Panorama," *Deseret Evening News*, December 12, 1879, and *Woman's Exponent*, December 15, 1879.

2. "1st Scene," Charles J. Christensen lecture, undated, MS 3149, Church History Library.

3. "The Panorama," *The Daily Ogden Junction*, February 12, 1880, 4.

4. *The Daily Ogden Junction*, October 18, 1880, 4.

5. Handbill, "Christensen's Grand Historical Exhibition," n.d., c. 1880, Res Nq M281 C554c 190-?, Church History Library.

6. Noel A. Carmack, "'One of the Most Interesting Seeneries That Can Be Found in Zion': Philo Dibble's Museum and Panorama," *Nauvoo Journal* (1997): 26–28. Dibble showed his panorama until the mid-1880s, although he felt that Christensen's Mormon Panorama imposed upon his trade. In 1879, Dibble wrote letters to President John Taylor complaining about Christensen's traveling performances. Philo Dibble to John Taylor, March 16 and April 29, 1879, Church History Library.

7. For more on American panoramas of the 1840s, see Joseph Earl Arrington, "Henry Lewis' Moving Panorama of the Mississippi River," *Louisiana History: The Journal of the Louisiana Historical Association* 6, no. 3 (Summer 1965): 239–272.

8. Carmack, "'One of the Most Interesting Seeneries," 25.

9. Richard L. Jensen and Richard G. Oman, *C. C. A. Christensen, 1831–1912: Mormon Immigrant Artist* (The Church of Jesus Christ of Latter-day Saints, 1984), 19.

10. See, for example, Genelle Pugmire, "Sunday Rally in Provo Supports Keeping Minerva Teichert Murals in the Manti Temple," *Daily Herald*, April

12, 2021; Trent Toone, "Church Will Try to Preserve Manti Temple's Minerva Teichert Murals," *Deseret News*, March 24, 2021. For more on Teichert's Manti Temple murals, see Doris R. Dant, "Minerva Teichert's Manti Temple Murals," *BYU Studies* 38, no. 3 (1999): 6–39.

11. See, for instance, Peggy Fletcher Stack, "Manti LDS Temple Reopens. Those Saved Minerva Teichert Murals Can Now Be Savored," *Salt Lake Tribune*, March 11, 2024; Jody England Hansen, "An Artist Story—How One Person Saved the Minerva Teichert Murals in the Manti Temple," *Exponent II* (blog), March 27, 2024, https://exponentii.org.

12. See, Marian Wardle, *Minerva Teichert: Pageants in Paint* (Brigham Young University Museum of Art, 2007); John W. Welch and Doris R. Dant, *The Book of Mormon Paintings of Minerva Teichert* (BYU Studies, 2009).

13. The Church of Jesus Christ of Latter-day Saints, "Gospel Art," *The Saints Crossing the Mississippi*, https://www.churchofjesuschrist.org/media/image/saints-crossing-the-mississippi-8d2c0d4; The Church of Jesus Christ of Latter-day Saints, "Gospel Art," *Handcart Pioneers*, https://www.churchofjesuschrist.org/media/image/handcart-pioneers-christensen-da14cd5; The Church of Jesus Christ of Latter-day Saints, "Gospel Art," *Winter Quarters*, https://www.churchofjesuschrist.org/media/image/winter-quarters-christensen-5b5ce15.

14. Located at Temple Square in Salt Lake City and owned by The Church of Jesus Christ of Latter-day Saints, the institution was later renamed the Church History Museum.

15. C. C. A. Christensen, mission journal dated January 23, 1853, to May 25, 1853, translated by Eva M. Gregersen and Orson B. West, as quoted in Marva O. and Eldred A. Johnson, *Carl Christian Anton Christensen, Elise Rosalia Sternheim Scheel Haarby, Maren Fredrikka Pettersen: The Story of Their Lives* (1999), M270.1 C554, Church History Library, 2.

16. C. C. A. Christensen reminiscences, MS 7383, Church History Library, 9; Christensen, mission journal dated January 23, 1853, to May 25, 1853, in Marva O. and Eldred A. Johnson, *Carl Christian Anton Christensen*, 4.

17. Christensen reminiscences, 8; Christensen, mission journal dated January 23, 1853, to May 25, 1853, in Marva O. and Eldred A. Johnson, *Carl Christian Anton Christensen*, 2–3.

18. Christensen reminiscences, 12; Christensen, mission journal dated January 23, 1853, to May 25, 1853, in Marva O. and Eldred A. Johnson, *Carl Christian Anton Christensen*, 4.

19. Christensen, mission journal dated January 23, 1853, to May 25, 1853, in Marva O. and Eldred A. Johnson, *Carl Christian Anton Christensen*, 7.

20. Aase Bak, "A Case Study of a Danish-American Artist: C. C. A. Christensen," in *From Scandinavia to America: Proceedings from a Conference held*

at Gl. Holtegaard, eds. Steffen Elmer Jørgensen, Lars Scheving, and Niels Peter Stilling (Odense University Press, 1987), 358.

21. For more on nineteenth-century Latter-day Saint formulations of apocalypse, Babylon, and the Kingdom of God, see Christopher James Blythe, *Terrible Revolution: Latter-day Saints and the American Apocalypse* (Oxford University Press, 2000).

22. Christensen, mission journal dated January 23, 1853, to May 25, 1853, translated by Eva M. Gregersen and Orson B. West, as quoted in Marva O. and Eldred A. Johnson, *Carl Christian Anton Christensen*, 8.

23. Christensen, mission journal dated January 23, 1853, to May 25, 1853, in Marva O. and Eldred A. Johnson, *Carl Christian Anton Christensen*, 8.

24. Andrew Jenson, *History of the Scandinavian Mission* (Deseret News Press, 1927), 96.

25. Reid L. Neilson and Scott D. Marianno, *Restless Pilgrim: Andrew Jenson's Quest for Latter-day Saint History* (University of Illinois Press, 2022), 27.

26. Christensen reminiscences, 13; Christensen, mission journal dated January 23, 1853, to May 25, 1853, in Marva O. and Eldred A. Johnson, *Carl Christian Anton Christensen*, 8.

27. Christensen, mission journal dated January 23, 1853, to May 25, 1853, in Marva O. and Eldred A. Johnson, *Carl Christian Anton Christensen*, 8.

28. Jenson, *History of the Scandinavian Mission*, 85.

29. Christensen reminiscences, 27–28; Jensen, *History of the Scandinavian Mission*, 92.

30. Jenson, *History of the Scandinavian Mission*, 94.

31. C. C. A. Christensen, "Early Missionary Experiences," *Juvenile Instructor* 31, no. 1 (January 1, 1896): 27.

32. "June 1854," C. C. A. Christensen, mission journal dated October 1853 to August 1854, translated by Orson B. West, as quoted in Marva O. and Eldred A. Johnson, *Carl Christian Anton Christensen*, 43.

33. "November 4, 1853," C. C. A. Christensen, mission journal dated October 1853 to August 1854, translated by Orson B. West, as quoted in Marva O. and Eldred A. Johnson, *Carl Christian Anton Christensen*, 32.

34. "August 4, 1854," C. C. A. Christensen, mission journal dated October 1853 to August 1854, translated by Orson B. West, as quoted in Marva O. and Eldred A. Johnson, *Carl Christian Anton Christensen*, 35.

35. "Carl Christian Anthon Christensen," Church History Biographical Database, https://history.churchofjesuschrist.org/chd/individual/carl-christian-anthon-christensen-1831.

36. Bernard Snow to Brigham Young, November 28, 1862, Brigham Young Collection, CR1234/1, Box 29, Folder 5 (Reel 40), Church History Library. With thanks to Ardis Parshall for bringing this letter to my attention.

37. Marva O. and Eldred A. Johnson, *Carl Christian Anton Christensen*, 58.

38. C. C. A. Christensen, "Going on a Mission Under Difficulties," *Juvenile Instructor* (May 15–June 15, 1902).

39. This is the first of three stanzas. C. C. A. Christensen, "Mon Hjemme i Dalen Jeg Savnes?" September 28, 1865, *Danish Hymnbook of The Church of Jesus Christ of Latter-day Saints*, translated by Richard L. Jensen, as quoted in Marva O. and Eldred A. Johnson, *Carl Christian Anton Christensen*, 70.

40. "Autobiography of Maren Fredrikka Pettersen," in Marva O. and Eldred A. Johnson, *Carl Christian Anton Christensen*, 145.

41. In one journal, Christensen recorded a ledger of wages and boarding costs at the railroad camp from December 1868 to February 1869. In a January 1869 poem, he listed himself in the John W. Young railroad camp in South Weber. Marva O. and Eldred A. Johnson, *Carl Christian Anton Christensen*, 83–84.

42. Richard L. Jensen and Richard G. Oman, "Oral History of Norma Christensen Taggart," typescript interview, *The James Moyle Oral History Program*, MS 200 708, Church History Library, February 1980, 39.

43. Their Manasseh log cabin is now on display in Ephraim as part of the Granary Arts complex.

44. Elise Christensen to C. C. A. Christensen, West Point, February 5, 1880, translated by Eldred A. Johnson, as quoted in Marva O. and Eldred A. Johnson, *Carl Christian Anton Christensen*, 135, 163–164.

45. John F. F. Dorius served time in federal prison in the late 1880s for unlawful cohabitation.

46. C. C. A. Christensen, journal dated 1875, quoted in Marva O. and Eldred A. Johnson, *Carl Christian Anton Christensen*, 89.

47. An 1878 report about this panorama says, "Its object is in missionary labors among the Lamanites or Indians to convey a clear and ready conception to their minds of leading events of sacred history" ("Pictorial Preaching," *Deseret News*, June 26, 1878). The historical record does not seem to indicate that many European Latter-day Saint settlers viewed this scroll. There may be another reference to Church members using this artwork as a visual aid to preach among local tribes, if it is the same work called "Judean Panorama Views" in an 1879 letter. This written request from Elder Edward Hunter to President John Taylor asks if "C. C. Christensen of Sanpete" can "borrow our Judean Panorama Views now in our office to present to the Indians of Thistle Valley" (First Presidency [John Taylor] correspondence, 1877–1887, CR 1 180, Church History Library). With thanks to Ardis Parshall for bringing this letter to my attention.

48. For more on the recovery of the Huntington Panorama, see Laura Allred Hurtado, "'It Is Priceless': C. C. A. Christensen's *Untitled [Huntington/Lamanite Panorama]*," *Pioneer* 66, no. 1 (2019): 8–15.

49. C. C. A Christensen to A. W. Winberg, *Bikuben*, March 20, 1879, quoted in Richard L. Jensen and Richard G. Oman, *C. C. A. Christensen, 1831–1912: Mormon Immigrant Artist* (The Church of Jesus Christ of Latter-day Saints, 1984), 18.

50. C. C. A. Christensen Journal, "A Mission to Scandinavia 1887–1889," MS d 7220, Box 2, Folder 2, v. 17, Church History Library.

51. "Church History," *Deseret News*, February 26, 1879.

52. "Mormon Panorama," *Deseret News*, September 18, 1883.

53. C. C. A. Christensen, "Correspondence, St. George, 25th July 1881," *Bikuben*, August 4, 1881, translated by Richard L. Jensen.

54. Edje Jeter, "Things I Did Not Know: Dinosaurs in the Manti Temple (Edit: New Images, ht Mina)," *Juvenile Instructor* (blog), August 4, 2013, https://juvenileinstructor.org. Minette Marcroft first pointed out the connection to Riou's illustrations in a comment on the above blog post in 2013.

55. "Louis Figuier," *Linda Hall Library*, November 8, 2022, https://lindahall.org.

56. Richard Somerset, "Textual Evolution: The Transformation of Louis Figuier's La Terra Avant le Deluge," *The Translator* 17, 2011: 255.

57. Louis Figuier, *The World Before the Deluge*, ed. H. W. Bristow (Cassell, Petter & Galpin, 1872), 53, 56, 172. Images available at https://www.gutenberg.org/ebooks/39723.

58. Figuier, *World Before the Deluge*, 190, 231, 241.

59. "November 8, 1887," C. C. A. Christensen, journals dated August 1887 to December 1889, MS 7220, Church History Library.

60. He commented on seeing the statue of "Liberty enlightening the world" as he left New York and noted he was "disappointed in the effect of impression it made on me, as far as Form and Beauty is connected with it" (August 30, 1887). He noted he was pleased with the Museum of Art and Zoology and Antiquity in Liverpool (September 10, 1887), the Grand Exposition of Arts and Industries in Denmark (May 18, 1888), the National Museum in Denmark (September 25, 1888), and the castle and crypt of Sønderborg (December 18, 1888). C. C. A. Christensen, journals dated August 1887 to December 1889, MS 7220, Church History Library.

61. C. C. A. Christensen to Elise and family from Copenhagen, September 21, 1888, translated by Kirsten Olsen, as quoted in Marva O. and Eldred A. Johnson, *Carl Christian Anton Christensen*, 166.

62. C. C. A. Christensen to Niels Erastus, February 9, 1889, as quoted in Marva O. and Eldred A. Johnson, *Carl Christian Anton Christensen*, 55, 168. The "Academy School" is likely the Sanpete Stake Academy (the forerunner of Snow College), which opened in Ephraim in 1888.

63. "July 4, 1889," C. C. A. Christensen, journals dated August 1887 to December 1889, MS 7220, Church History Library.

64. C. C. A. Christensen to Elise, August 13, 1889, as quoted in Marva O. and Eldred A. Johnson, *Carl Christian Anton Christensen*, 174.

65. *Sanpete County Register*, Ephraim, July 3, 1890.

66. "C. C. A. Christensen and Family at Provo, Thurs., April 22," *Sanpete County Register*, Ephraim, April 22, 1891.

67. *The Manti Sentinel*, October 19, 1894.

68. The famous Danish fairy tale author Hans Christian Andersen.

69. Carl Christian Anton Christensen, "Gammelt Junk [Old Rubbish]," translated by R. Wayne Stoker, *Family Search*, January 2020.

Chapter Two. Israelite Wilderness and American Frontier

1. For more on the Paris Art Mission, see Linda Jones Gibbs, "The Paris Art Mission," in *Latter-day Saint Art: A Critical Reader*, eds. Amanda Beardsley and Mason Kamana Allred (Oxford University Press, 2024) and Linda Jones Gibbs, *Harvesting the Light: The Paris Art Mission and Beginnings of Utah Impressionism* (The Church of Jesus Christ of Latter-day Saints, 1987).

2. Image available at https://www.metmuseum.org/art/collection/search/729621.

3. *The Divine Comedy of Dante Alighieri: Inferno*, trans. Allen Mandelbaum, vol. 1 (Bantam Dell, 2004), 2.

4. Robert Pogue Harrison, *Forests: The Shadow of Civilization* (The University of Chicago Press, 1992), 82–83.

5. Harrison, *Forests*, 84, 178.

6. Roderick Frazier Nash, *Wilderness and the American Mind*, 5th ed. (Yale University Press, 2014), xx–xxii, 1–2, 9.

7. Perry Miller, *Errand into the Wilderness* (The Belknap Press of Harvard University Press, 1956), 115–116.

8. Hugh Nibley, *An Approach to the Book of Mormon* (Deseret News Press, 1957), 124–125.

9. Nash, *Wilderness*, 2–3, 13–14.

10. With thanks to Samuel Brown for thoughts on forests and wilderness in the Book of Mormon.

11. John L. Marsh, "Drama and Spectacle by the Yard: The Panorama in America," *Journal of Popular Culture* 10, no. 3 (Winter 1976): 581–582.

12. Nenette Luarca-Shoaf, "Excavating a Nineteenth-Century Mass Medium," *American Art* 27, no. 2 (Summer 2013): 15–20. The work is titled *Panorama of the Monumental Grandeur of the Mississippi Valley* and is the only surviving example of the several Mississippi River panoramas.

13. Dawn Pheysey, "Armchair Travel: The Moving Panorama," unpublished manuscript for "Passion for Place Symposium," Brigham Young University Museum of Art curatorial files, 11.

14. For more on the Philo Dibble panorama and a comparison of its scenes with those in Christensen's Mormon Panorama, see, R. Devan Jensen, "Philo Dibble's Dream of 'A Gallery in Zion,'" *Journal of Mormon History* 44, no. 4 (2018): 19–39.

15. Donna L. Poulton, *Reuben Kirkham: Pioneer Artist* (Cedar Fort, Inc., 2011).

16. As noted by R. Devan Jensen in "From the Diary of Frederick Kesler: Baptism of American Indians at Dimick B. Huntington's Property" in *Pioneer* 66, no. 1 (2019), 7, the panorama's presentation to Indigenous people was recorded in the diary of Frederick Kesler on March 19, 1875: "Prst Young & his Councilers met in council with the Lamanites in our ward School House[.] 50 or 60 indians ware presant[.] a few of our Breathern ware presant[.] a Small panarama got up by D. B. Huntington was exibited commencing with adam & eve in the garden of Eaden with several interesting circumstances or insidences which transpired from then until the time that the angle moroni delivered the plates unto Joseph Smith. each picture was Exsplained unto them. they ware verry mutch interest[ed]." *Diary of Frederick Kesler, 1874–1877*, J. Willard Marriott Library, University of Utah. See, Jonathan Stapley, "From the Archives: Native Americans and Frederick Kesler," *Juvenile Instructor* (blog), December 4, 2013, https://juvenileinstructor.org.

17. Similarly, in 1888, Andrew Jenson was sent a mission by Church leaders to tour historic sites of the Restoration in New York, Ohio, Missouri, and Illinois and then prepare a written history documenting persecution of the Saints and the lack of protection from the government. Upon his return to Utah, Jenson also lectured publicly on this history with commissioned paintings of the sites. See, Reid L. Neilson and Scott D. Marianno, *Restless Pilgrim: Andrew Jenson's Quest for Latter-day Saint History* (University of Illinois Press, 2022), 124–129.

18. *Pioneer* 66, no. 1 (2019), 19.

19. Henry Nash Smith, *Virgin Land: The American West as Symbol and Myth* (Harvard University Press, 1950), 215.

20. Nash, *Wilderness*, 35.

21. Nash, *Wilderness*, 43.

22. See, Jennifer Champoux, "'In Their Promised Canaan Stand': Outlawry, Landscape, and Memory in C. C. A. Christensen's Mormon Panorama," *BYU Studies Quarterly* 60, no. 2 (2021): 4–48.

23. This scene is no longer extant, but its subject is described in surviving versions of the lecture script that Christensen or his son read during presentations of the panorama. Charles J. Christensen lecture, undated, MS 3149, Church History Library.

24. Tellingly, the Latin word for "left" is *sinister*.

25. Milton V. Backman Jr., "Awakenings in the Burned-Over District: New Light on the Historical Setting of the First Vision," *BYU Studies* 9, no. 3 (1969): 306.

26. Brett Malcolm Grainger, *Church in the Wild: Evangelicals in Antebellum America* (Harvard University Press, 2019), 22. See also Russell E. Richey, *Methodism in the American Forest* (Oxford University Press, 2015).

27. Image available at https://www.metmuseum.org/art/collection/search/336222.

28. Joseph Smith—History 1:14.

29. Jan Shipps and John Welch, eds., *The Journals of William E. McLellin, 1831–1836* (Brigham Young University Studies, 1994), 177, entry for May 14, 1835. With thanks to Samuel Brown for this reference.

30. *Times and Seasons* 2/1 (1 Nov 1840), 204. With thanks to Samuel Brown for this reference.

31. Grainger, *Church in the Wild*, 30, 33.

32. Christopher James Blythe, *Terrible Revolution: Latter-day Saints and the American Apocalypse* (Oxford University Press, 2020), 119–122.

33. Charles J. Christensen lecture, undated, "Crossing the Missippi [*sic*] On the Ice," MS 3149, Church History Library.

34. See Exodus 16:13–15; Richard L. Jensen and Richard G. Oman, *C. C. A. Christensen, 1831–1912: Mormon Immigrant Artist* (The Church of Jesus Christ of Latter-day Saints, 1984), 110.

35. Charles J. Christensen lecture, undated, "Catching Quails," MS 3149, Church History Library.

36. 1 Nephi 16:14.

37. 1 Nephi 16:16.

38. 1 Nephi 17:2, 12.

39. 1 Nephi 18:25.

40. Gustav H. Blanke with Karen Lynn, "'God's Base of Operations': Mormon Variations on the American Sense of Mission," *BYU Studies* 20, no. 1 (1979): 90.

41. Lehi's vision of the tree of life appears in 1 Nephi 8.

42. Jacob 5.

43. Helaman 3:5.

44. Enos 1:20–21.

45. Smith, *Virgin Land*, 123.

46. Nash, *Wilderness*, 33.

47. William W. Phelps, "The Elders in the Land of Zion to the Church of Christ Scattered Abroad, *Evening and the Morning Star* 1 (July 1832): 5.

48. Sarah Dant, "The 'Lion of the Lord' and the Land: Brigham Young's Environmental Ethic," in *The Earth Will Appear as the Garden of Eden: Essays on Mormon Environmental History*, eds. Jedediah S. Rogers and Matthew C. Godfrey (The University of Utah Press, 2019), 33. See also Godfrey, "The Natural World and the Establishment of Zion, 1831–1833," in *The Earth Will Appear as the Garden of Eden: Essays on Mormon Environmental History*, eds. Jedediah S. Rogers and Matthew C. Godfrey (The University of Utah Press, 2019), 76.

49. Godfrey, "The Natural World," 71.

50. Nash, *Wilderness*, 43, 47, 66–67.

51. Helaman 3:9.

52. Steven C. Harper, *First Vision: Memory and Mormon Origins* (Oxford University Press, 2019), 111.

Chapter Three. Old World Style and New World Scripture

1. The earliest Book of Mormon paintings were part of a small panorama made by C. C. A. Christensen in the early 1870s. As discussed in chapter two, the panorama was a visual aid to assist Latter-day Saint missionaries preaching to the Ute and Shoshone people in Utah. Another very early Book of Mormon painting was done in 1875 by David Hyrum Smith (the youngest son of Joseph and Emma Smith and a leader in the Reorganized Church of Jesus Christ of Latter Day Saints in Illinois) with a scene of Lehi's dream from 1 Nephi 8. In 1883, Reuben Kirkham painted twenty-three scenes (now lost) in his Book of Mormon panorama. Other early Book of Mormon images appeared in 1888 when George Reynolds published *The Story of the Book of Mormon*, with fourteen illustrations by Salt Lake City artists George Ottinger, William Armitage, John Held Sr., and William C. Morris.

2. "To the Artists of Utah (March 8, 1890)," *Deseret Weekly*, March 8, 1890, 367.

3. Richard L. Jensen and Richard G. Oman, *C. C. A. Christensen, 1831–1912: Mormon Immigrant Artist* (The Church of Jesus Christ of Latter-day Saints, 1984), 63. Some of the lithographs are marked "VANDERCOOK-Co. CHI."

4. *Sanpete County Register* (Ephraim City, Utah), July 3, 1890, and *Sanpete County Register* (Ephraim City, Utah), October 9, 1890.

5. With thanks to Ardis Parshall for this insight. The film's scene of Nephi's vision essentially copies Christensen's *Nephi's Vision*, with an angel pointing and Nephi looking toward an iconic virgin and child in the background. See William A. Morton, *Nephi's Vision*, 1915, film still, The Book of Mormon Art Catalog, https://bookofmormonartcatalog.org/catalog/nephis-vision-2/. See also, Ardis E. Parshall, "Mormon Movies: Life of Nephi, 1915," *The Keepapitchinin* (blog), February 6, 2018, http://www.keepapitchinin.org.

6. Jennifer Champoux, "'In Their Promised Canaan Stand': Outlawry, Landscape, and Memory in C. C. A. Christensen's Mormon Panorama," *BYU Studies Quarterly* 60, no. 2 (2021): 9.

7. Anna Schram Vejlby, "Hiding in Plain Sight: History Painting as a National Genre," in *Danish Golden Age*, exh. cat. (Stockholm: Nationalmuseum, 2019), 134.

8. C. C. A. Christensen, journals dated 1853–1889, August 1887–December 1889, MS 7220, Church History Library.

9. In the collection of The Museum of National History at Frederiksborg Castle. Image available at https://commons.wikimedia.org/wiki/File:Bloch-SermonOnTheMount.jpg.

10. For an example of the style of earlier Danish history painting, see, Christian August Lorentzen's *The Most Terrible Night. View of Kongens Nytorv in Copenhagen During the English Bombardment of Copenhagen at Night between 4 and 5 September 1807* (1808), in the collection of the Statens Museum for Kunst.

11. Noel A. Carmack, "'A Picturesque and Dramatic History:' George Reynolds's Story of the Book of Mormon," *BYU Studies* 47, no. 2 (2008): 118, 124, 132.

12. Heidi S. Clausen (Danish National Archives) to Jay M. Todd (*Ensign* magazine), December 10, 1990, CR 215 11, Church History Library.

13. Aase Bak, "A Case Study of a Danish-American Artist: C. C. A. Christensen," in *From Scandinavia to America: Proceedings from a Conference held at Gl. Holtegaard*, eds. Steffen Elmer Jørgensen, Lars Scheving, and Niels Peter Stilling (Odense University Press, 1987), 358.

14. This trend began when Doyle L. Green, the managing editor of the Church magazine *Improvement Era*, published several of Bloch's images of Christ in *Improvement Era* in the late 1950s. For more on the lasting influence of Christensen and Bloch, see James R. Swensen, "Two Danish Artists—Two Not So Divergent Paths: C. C. A. Christensen, Carl Bloch, and the Evolution of Latter-day Saint Art and Aesthetics," *The Journal of Mormon History* 49, no. 2 (2023): 107–120.

15. See, "Lehi Preaching to the Jews," *Juvenile Instructor*, April 15, 1891; "Lehi and His Family in the Wilderness," *Juvenile Instructor*, May 1, 1891; "Nephi and

Zoram with the Records," *Juvenile Instructor*, May 15, 1891; "The Peacemakers," *Juvenile Instructor*, June 1, 1891; "Nephi's Vision," *Juvenile Instructor*, June 15, 1891; "Lehi Finding the Liahona," *Juvenile Instructor*, July 1, 1891; "The Building of the Ship," *Juvenile Instructor*, July 15, 1891; "Lehi Offering Sacrifice," *Juvenile Instructor*, August 1, 1891; "Lehi Blessing His Posterity," *Juvenile Instructor*, August 15, 1891; "The Nephites Seeking a New Home," *Juvenile Instructor*, September 1, 1891; "The Building of the Temple," *Juvenile Instructor*, September 15, 1891; and "Nephi Making the Plates," *Juvenile Instructor*, October 1, 1891.

16. Like his compatriot Carl Bloch, Bertel Thorvaldsen has an unexpected connection to the Church. A replica of his 1821–1823 *Christus* statue was used to represent the Church in the 1964 New York World's Fair. Today, replicas of Thorvaldsen's *Christus* are placed in many Temple Visitors' Centers, and the statue is the basis for the official Church logo.

17. C. C. A. Christensen, journals dated 1853–1889, July–September 1865, MS 7220, Church History Library.

18. C. C. A. Christensen, journals dated 1853–1889, July–September 1865.

19. Jensen and Oman, *C. C. A. Christensen*, 64.

20. In the collection of the Statens Museum for Kunst.

21. Karina Lykke Grand, "Defining the Golden Age: The History of an Epoch and a Concept," in *Danish Golden Age*, exh. cat. (Stockholm: Nationalmuseum, 2019), 44.

22. See, for example, Constantin Hansen, *Danish Artists in Rome*, 1837, or Martinus Rørbye, *View from the Artist's Window*, 1825, both in the Statens Museum for Kunst.

23. "To the Artists of Utah," *Deseret Weekly*, 367.

24. Nathan Rees, *Mormon Visual Culture and the American West* (Routledge, 2021), 13.

25. Edward Said, *Orientalism* (Pantheon Books, 1978), 2–3.

26. Vernet painted a complex "friendship portrait" of Thorvaldsen working on a sculpted bust of Vernet in 1833, which is today in the Thorvaldsens Museum.

27. Linda Nochlin, "The Imaginary Orient," *Art in America* 71, no. 5 (May 1983): 122.

28. See, Jennifer R. Henneman, ed., *Near East to Far West: Fictions of French and American Colonialism* (Yale University Press, 2023).

29. An 1840 engraved copy by Hipolyte Lecomte of Vernet's painting is in the collection of The Metropolitan Museum of Art. Image available at https://www.metmuseum.org/art/collection/search/811435.

30. Jennifer Henneman, "Near East to Far West: Fictions of French and American Colonialism," in *Near East to Far West: Fictions of French and*

American Colonialism, ed. Jennifer R. Henneman (Yale University Press, 2023), 22.

31. Image available at https://bookofmormonartcatalog.org/catalog/vision-of-nephi/.

32. Noel A. Carmack, "'A Picturesque and Dramatic History,'" 130.

33. This painting's fame is due in part to its relocation to Germany in 1754 and to the discussion of it in Johann Joachim Winckelmann's *The History of the Art of Antiquity*, a foundational text for the study of art.

34. 1 Nephi 11:14.

35. Edgar Garcia, "Moroni's Body; Or, The Skins of Moroni," Roundtable essays on "Mormonism, Race, and the History of Sexuality," *American Religion*, April 11, 2022, american-religion.org/mormons-race-sexuality/garcia.

36. Richard Oman, "'Ye Shall See the Heavens Open': Portrayal of the Divine and the Angelic in Latter-day Saint Art," *BYU Studies Quarterly* 35, no. 4 (1995): 125.

37. For a discussion on Cannon's 1883 comments about wings on angels in art, see Nathan Rees, *Mormon Visual Culture*, 25.

38. Marva O. and Eldred A. Johnson, *Carl Christian Anton Christensen, Elise Rosalia Sternheim Scheel Haarby, Maren Fredrikka Pettersen: The Story of Their Lives* (1999), M270.1 C554, Church History Library, 330–333.

39. C. C. A. Christensen, journals dated 1853–1889, MS 7220, Church History Library, 410.

40. C. C. A. Christensen, journals dated 1853–1889, 420.

41. Marva O. and Eldred A. Johnson, *Carl Christian Anton Christensen*, 323.

42. A similar attention to detail in ship-building techniques is apparent in Danish art of the 1820s and 1830s. Those decades saw a flurry of ship construction following the destruction of the Danish fleet by the British in 1807. At the time, artists from the Royal Danish Academy captured scenes of ship building. See, for example, Martinus Rørbye, *Artists Painting by a Shipyard* of 1826 (Statens Museum for Kunst). Karina Lykke Grand, "Defining the Golden Age: The History of an Epoch and a Concept," in *Danish Golden Age*, exh. cat. (Stockholm: Nationalmuseum, 2019), 35.

43. Richard L. Jensen and C. C. A. Christensen, "C. A. A. Christensen on Art: from the Salt Lake City Bikuben February–March 1892," *BYU Studies* 23, no. 4 (Fall 1983): 406.

44. Jensen and Christensen, "C. C. A. Christensen on Art," 408.

45. Jensen and Christensen, "C. C. A. Christensen on Art," 410–411.

46. For example, on 15 August 1867, Christensen wrote that he "bore my Testemony [*sic*] to the Truth as revealed through the prophet Joseph etc." Again,

in November 1888, he wrote that he had "born my testimony to the Truth of God's Work, and in particular to the Book of Mormon." C. C. A. Christensen, journals dated 1853–1889, Typescripts of volumes 1–17, MS 7220, Church History Library, 317–423.

Chapter Four. Envisioning Zion

1. "Official Declaration 1," https://www.churchofjesuschrist.org/study/scriptures/dc-testament/od/1?lang=eng.

2. Matthew Bowman, *The Mormon People: The Making of An American Faith* (Random House, 2012), 153.

3. C. C. A. Christensen, "Lovpriser vor Frelser med Jubel og Sang," trans. Eldred A. Johnson, in Marva O. and Eldred A. Johnson, *Carl Christian Anton Christensen, Elise Rosalia Sternheim Scheel Haarby, Maren Fredrikka Pettersen: The Story of Their Lives* (1999), M270.1 C554, Church History Library, 11–12.

4. John Taylor, "The Kingdom of God or Nothing," Nov 1, 1857, *Journal of Discourses*, 6:21–22. For more on nineteenth-century Latter-day Saint formulations of identity as a chosen people restoring righteousness and freedom, see Jennifer Champoux, "'In Their Promised Canaan Stand': Outlawry, Landscape, and Memory in C. C. A. Christensen's Mormon Panorama," *BYU Studies Quarterly* 60, no. 2 (2021): 4–48; David W. Grua, "Memoirs of the Persecuted: Persecution, Memory, and the West as a Mormon Refuge" (master's thesis, Brigham Young University, 2008); and Steven C. Harper, *First Vision: Memory and Mormon Origins* (Oxford University Press, 2019).

5. As translated in Marva O. and Eldred A. Johnson, *Carl Christian Anton Christensen*, 336–337.

6. Julie K. Allen, *Danish but Not Lutheran: The Impact of Mormonism on Danish Cultural Identity, 1850–1920* (The University of Utah Press, 2017), 8, 59.

7. Reid L. Neilson and Scott D. Marianno, *Restless Pilgrim: Andrew Jenson's Quest for Latter-day Saint History* (University of Illinois Press, 2022), 36.

8. *Millennial Star*, April 4, 1868, no. 14: 221–222.

9. C. C. A. Christensen, "Vor er vel Zion, Herrens Stad? [Where is Zion, the Lord's City?]," trans. R. Wayne Stoker, *Family Search*, 2020, with edits by Jennifer Champoux, 2024.

10. Julie K. Allen, "Mormonism, Gender, and Art in Nineteenth-Century Scandinavia," in *The Routledge Handbook of Mormonism and Gender*, eds. Taylor G. Petrey and Amy Hoyt (Routledge, 2020), 119, quoting from Jørgen W. Schmidt's *C. C. A. Christensen: Dansk-americansk maler, digter, samfundsrevser og missionaer [Danish-American painter, poet, social reformer and missionary]* (Forlaget Moroni, 1984), 32.

11. W. Paul Reeve, *Religion of a Different Color: Race and the Mormon Struggle for Whiteness* (Oxford University Press, 2015), 4, 8, 43.

12. J. Spencer Fluhman, *"A Peculiar People" Anti-Mormonism and the Making of Religion in Nineteenth-Century America* (The University of North Carolina Press, 2012), 103–104.

13. Nathan Rees, *Mormon Visual Culture and the American West* (Routledge, 2021), 41.

14. For a detailed history of Mormon-Native relations in Utah, see Jared Farmer, *On Zion's Mount: Mormons, Indians, and the American Landscape* (Harvard University Press, 2008).

15. Scott R. Christensen, *Sagwitch: Shoshone Chieftain, Mormon Elder, 1822–1887* (Utah State University Press, 1999), 88–89.

16. Christensen, *Sagwitch*, 90.

17. Christensen, *Sagwitch*, 104.

18. Dimick B. Huntington to Joseph F. Smith, 6 Jun 1875, in *Millennial Star*, July 6, 1875, 426, as quoted in R. Devan Jensen, Scott R. Christensen, and Darren Parry, "'Like Fire in the Dry Grass': Shoshone Conversions and the Christensen Teaching Scroll," *Pioneer* 66, no. 1 (2019): 43.

19. Christensen, *Sagwitch*, 140–182.

20. As quoted in Jensen, Christensen, and Parry, "Like Fire in the Dry Grass," 19; *Diary of Frederick Kesler, 1874–1877*, J. Willard Marriott Library, University of Utah.

21. Interview with Mrs. Charles W. Hill, Charles E. Dibble, 30 July 1945 (Reminiscences relating to her father-in-law, George W. Hill and the missions to the Indians in early Utah and Idaho History), https://mendonutah.org/history/indians/indian-white-rel.htm.

22. For more on this tension, see Rees, *Mormon Visual Culture*, 40–61.

23. For a comparison of the versions by Christensen and McGahey, see Laura Allred Hurtado and David G., "Painting the Mythical and the Heroic: *Joseph Preaches to the American Indians*," *Juvenile Instructor* (blog), November 19, 2013, https://juvenileinstructor.org.

24. Joseph Smith, History, 1838–1856, August 12, 1841, The Joseph Smith Papers.

25. Laura Allred Hurtado and David G., "Painting the Mythical and the Heroic."

26. Reeve, *Religion of a Different Color*, 59.

27. Reeve, *Religion of a Different Color*, 75.

28. Jensen and Oman note that Hancock exhibited a panorama in Utah in 1883 and date these Christensen images to c. 1882–1884 (Richard L. Jensen and Richard G. Oman, *C. C. A. Christensen, 1831–1912: Mormon Immigrant Artist*

[The Church of Jesus Christ of Latter-day Saints, 1984], 86). However, an article in the *Sanpete County Register, Ephraim*, on February 26, 1891, titled "Ephraim's Artist," reads, "For some eight weeks the veteran painter, C. C. A. Christensen, has been engaged upon a panoramic series of early Utah and Mormon scenes . . . They are mostly views of early days of Missouri and Southern Utah and represent scenes of carnage and bloodshed, the chief actor being Mr. Hancock of Harrisville, for whom they were painted. The list of those so far done is: 'The bull fight on Peder River, Burning of the Morley settlement in Missouri, Burning of the Hancock Farm, Destruction of the Press at Independence, Killing of Joseph Smith, the Hancock family Leaving Missouri, Arrest of Walker." Based on this source, I date the Hancock Panorama to 1891.

29. For more on the Walker War and these images, see R. Devan Jensen, Scott R. Christensen, and Darren Parry, "Recently Discovered C. C. A. Christensen Panoramas and Indigenous Life in Utah," *Utah Historical Quarterly* (forthcoming).

30. Jensen and Oman, *C. C. A. Christensen*, 89.

31. The event depicted actually occurred on September 26, 1853.

32. Jensen and Oman, *C. C. A. Christensen*, 90.

33. The Chicago jury did not choose the piece for display at the Exposition.

34. Reeve, *Religion of a Different Color*, 79.

35. See Ashlee Whitaker Evans's discussion of these two paintings in "Establishing Zion: Identity and *Communitas* in Early Latter-day Saint Art," in *Latter-day Saint Art: A Critical Reader*, eds. Amanda Beardsley and Mason Kamana Allred (Oxford University Press, 2024), 111–112.

36. Carlyle Constantino also noted this shift between the two paintings in "Native Americans, Mormonism, and Art," in *Latter-day Saint Art: A Critical Reader*, eds. Amanda Beardsley and Mason Kamana Allred (Oxford University Press, 2024), 462.

37. "The Scandinavian Element," *Deseret News*, July 7, 1886, 6–7.

38. Epistle from the First Presidency, "To the Swedish Saints: Instructions in Regard to the Holding of Meetings, Amusements, Social Gatherings, etc.," 1901, as quoted in William Mulder, "Scandinavian Saga," in *The Peoples of Utah*, ed. Helen Z. Papanikolas (Utah State Historical Society, 1976). For more on the experience of Scandinavians in early Utah, see William Mulder, *Homeward to Zion: The Mormon Migration from Scandinavia* (University of Minnesota Press, 1957).

39. Allen, *Danish but Not Lutheran*, 203–204; Neilson and Marianno, *Restless Pilgrim*, 69.

40. The Scandinavian Heritage Festival still draws upwards of 10,000 visitors to Ephraim every May.

41. Neilson and Marianno, *Restless Pilgrim*, 206.

42. William Mulder, *"Man Kalder Mig Digter": C. C. A. Christensen, Poet of the Scandinavian Scene in Early Utah* (Utah Humanities Research Foundation, 1947), as quoted in Marva O. and Eldred A. Johnson, *Carl Christian Anton Christensen*, 115.

43. Marva O. and Eldred A. Johnson, *Carl Christian Anton Christensen,* 119.

44. C. C. A. Christensen, "Old Affections Don't Wear Out," *Bikuben*, May 2, 1912, translated by Eldred A. Johnson and quoted in Marva O. and Eldred A. Johnson, *Carl Christian Anton Christensen,* 126.

45. For more on Jenson's work, see Neilson and Marianno, *Restless Pilgrim*.

46. Andrew Jenson, *History of the Scandinavian Mission* (Deseret News Press, 1927), 91.

47. C. C. A. Christensen, "Early Missionary Experiences," *Juvenile Instructor* 30, no. 14, July 15, 1895.

48. C. C. A. Christensen, "Love Will Never Grow Old," 1901, in *Compiled information about C. C. A. Christensen* by Julia Rachel Olsen Davis, MS 7542 (Reel), Church History Library.

Bibliographic Essay

1. Christensen's unknown or nonextant works include the first scene of the Mormon Panorama showing Joseph Smith's vision of God the Father and His Son; a mural in the Ephraim tabernacle of Joseph Smith and the angel Moroni on the Hill Cumorah (of which a photograph exists); stage painting at the Springville Theater and Salt Lake Theater; murals in the St. George Temple (lost during the 1930s renovations); a fourth panorama of "Curious Ways, Manner and Customs of Various Countries" painted with Dan Weggeland and referred to by C. C. A.'s brother Mads Frederick in his autobiography and in a November 1879 *Deseret News* report; and decorative art such as signs, mantels, toys, and scenes on window blinds.

2. One handbill advertising a presentation of the Mormon Panorama included a testimonial from Church President John Taylor and other leaders. Handbill, "Christensen's Grand Historical Exhibition," n.d, c. 1880, Res Nq M281 C554c 190–?, Church History Library.

3. The Church of Jesus Christ of Latter-day Saints, Church History—All Gospel Art, https://www.churchofjesuschrist.org/media/collection/church-history-all-gospel-art-images.

4. "September 8–14: Doctrine and Covenants 98–101," and "September 15–21: Doctrine and Covenants 102–105," *Come, Follow Me—For Individual and Families: Doctrine and Covenants 2025*. These same two images were used in the same lessons in the 2021 version of the manual.

5. The Church of Jesus Christ of Latter-day Saints, "The Journey of Lehi's Family," https://history.churchofjesuschrist.org/exhibit/journey-of-lehis-family and "From Plates to Pages: Writing and Reading the Book of Mormon," https://history.churchofjesuschrist.org/exhibit/book-of-mormon-from-plates-to-pages.

6. The Church of Jesus Christ of Latter-day Saints, Museum Store Art Catalog, https://history.churchofjesuschrist.org/exhibit/museum-art-catalog-alphabetical?.

7. Written in Danish, these letters were preserved by Rachel Olsen Davis (daughter of Elise's oldest daughter, Eliza Virginia) and translated by Kirsten Olsen and Eldred A. Johnson.

8. C. C. A. Christensen correspondence, translated by Eldred A. Johnson, MS 5488, Church History Library.

9. These versions include a transcript in the Church History Library that is partially handwritten and partially typed, a typescript "Lectures as Written by C. C. A. Christensen" at the Brigham Young University L. Tom Perry Special Collections, and a computer typescript "Abbreviated Script / C. C. A. Christensen's Mormon Panorama," which is at the Brigham Young University Museum of Art and appears to be copied from the Special Collections version. None of these three sources indicates a date or provenance. Jennett Labrum, granddaughter of Seymour Christensen who donated the Mormon Panorama to BYU, provided the author with a slightly different typed script, but it appears to be of a later creation date as it incorporates the margin notes from the Church History Library version into the text parenthetically, it is missing two of the scenes, and it mentions Seymour at the end. The Museum of Art also has a typescript donated by the Christensen family, "Mormon Panorama Lectures of C. C. A. Christensen (as Written by Charles J. Christensen, Eldest Son of C. C. A. Christensen)," with a written note saying, "Copied from lecture script donated to MOA from Christensen family." This version has the most differences in wording, as compared with all the other versions, although they are mostly minor, and the substance is still mostly similar. All extant versions of the script follow a similar narrative, with only slight differences in details or wording.

10. C. C. A. Christensen journals, 1853–1889, MS 7220, Church History Library.

11. Compare, for example, the August 7, 1887, entry in "Notebook, 1881–1884" and "Journal, 1887 August–1889 December."

12. C. C. A. Christensen reminiscences, undated, MS 7383, Church History Library.

13. C. C. A. Christensen, "De skjønne Kunster," *Bikuben*, February 18 and 25 and March 3 and 31, 1892.

14. Richard L. Jensen and C. C. A. Christensen, "C. A. A. Christensen on Art," 405.

15. Jensen and Christensen, "C. A. A. Christensen on Art," 406.

16. Jensen and Christensen, "C. A. A. Christensen on Art," 406–413.

17. Jensen and Christensen, "C. A. A. Christensen on Art," 406.

18. See, for example, Lewis Henry Morgan's *Ancient Society*, published in 1877, which asserted three stages of social evolution: savagery, barbarism, and civilization.

19. Jensen and Christensen, "C. A. A. Christensen on Art," 406–407.

20. Jensen and Christensen, "C. A. A. Christensen on Art," 414.

21. Jensen and Christensen, "C. A. A. Christensen on Art," 415–416.

22. C. C. A. Christensen, "Early Missionary Experiences," published serially in *Juvenile Instructor*, June 15, 1895, to February 1, 1896.

23. C. C. A. Christensen, "Early Missionary Experiences," *Juvenile Instructor*, August 1, 1895: 461.

24. See, C. C. A. Christensen, "Going on a Mission Under Difficulties" published serially in *Juvenile Instructor*, May 15, 1902, to June 15, 1902; "C. C. N. Dorius," *Bikuben*, March 22, 1894; "Haandkarre-Sang fra 1857 [Handcart Song from 1857]," *Bikuben*, September 23, 1896; "Et Mindeblad til afdode Soster Laura A. Larsen" [A Page in Memory of Deceased Sister Laura A. Larsen], *Bikuben*, February 20, 1902; "Erindringer fra 1857" [Memories of 1857], *Bikuben*, October 1 and 8, 1903; "Over Praerierne," *Bikuben*, Sept 8, 1910; "CCA Christensen correspondence," *Bikuben*, September 15, 1904. For a translation and synthesis of some of these accounts, see Richard L. Jensen, translator, "By Handcart to Utah: The Account of C. C. A. Christensen," *Nebraska History* 66 (1985): 332–348.

25. Richard L. Jensen, "By Handcart to Utah: The Account of C. C. A. Christensen," 342.

26. See, Jennifer Champoux, "'In Their Promised Canaan Stand': Outlawry, Landscape, and Memory in C. C. A. Christensen's Mormon Panorama," *BYU Studies Quarterly* 60, no. 2 (2021): 4–48.

27. Jennett Labrum, email to author, 22 April 2021.

28. Charles J. Christensen lecture, undated, "Haun's Mill," MS 3149, Church History Library.

29. John L. Marsh, "Drama and Spectacle by the Yard: The Panorama in America," *Journal of Popular Culture* 10, no. 3 (Winter 1976): 585.

30. Richard L. Jensen and Richard G. Oman, *C. C. A. Christensen*.

31. Joseph F. Smith to C. C. A. Christensen, November 16, 1906, as quoted in in Marva O. and Eldred A. Johnson, *Carl Christian Anton Christensen, Elise*

Rosalia Sternheim Scheel Haarby, Maren Fredrikka Pettersen: The Story of Their Lives (1999), M270.1 C554, Church History Library, 147.

32. "Patriarch C. C. A. Christensen," *Bikuben*, April 13, 1911.

33. "One of the Church's Great Ones: Poet, Missionary and Writer, Artist, C. C. A. Christensen Lays Down the Earthly Envelope," *Bikuben*, July 11, 1912.

34. *The Home Sentinel*, Manti, September 4, 1885.

35. "Mormon Panorama," *Deseret News*, September 18, 1883.

36. "'Mormon' Panorama," *The Ogden Herald*, April 18, 1885.

37. John S. Hansen, ed., *Mindeudgave: C. C. A. Christensen: Poetiske Arbejder Artikler og Afhandlinger; tilligemed hans Levnedsløb* (Commemorative edition: C. C. A. Christensen: Poetic Works Articles and Treatises; also His Life), 1921, trans. Eldred A. Johnson in Marva O. and Eldred A. Johnson, *Carl Christian Anton Christensen*, 127.

38. William Mulder, "'Man Kalder Mig Digter': C. C. A. Christensen, Poet of the Scandinavian Scene in Early Utah," *Utah Humanities Review* (January 1947): 8–17.

39. Carl Carmer, "'Here Is My Home at Last!'" *American Heritage* (February 1963): 27–33, 98–102.

40. Carl Carmer, "A Panorama of Mormon Life," *Art in America* (May-June 1970): 52–65.

41. "Christensen: A Panorama of Mormon Life," August 13-September 7, 1970, curated by John I. H. Baur.

42. Richard L. Jensen and Richard G. Oman, *Oral History of Norma Christensen Taggart*, typescript interview (Salt Lake City, Utah, February 1980, The James Moyle Oral History Program), MS 200 708, Church History Library, 31.

43. Jane Dillenberger, "Mormonism and American Religious Art," *Sunstone* 3 (May/June 1978): 13–17.

44. Jensen and Oman, *C. C. A. Christensen*.

45. "On the Road with C. C. A. Christensen: The Moving Panorama," March 6-September 8, 2003, curated by Dawn Pheysey.

46. "On the Road with C. C. A. Christensen: The Moving Panorama," exhibition brochure, Brigham Young University Museum of Art, 2003.

47. R. Scott Lloyd, "Vivid Panorama: C. C. A. Christensen Recreation Perpetuates Artist's Legacy," *Church News*, June 11, 2005.

48. Noel A. Carmack, "'A Picturesque and Dramatic History:' George Reynolds's Story of the Book of Mormon," *BYU Studies* 47, no. 2 (2008): 115–141; "'One of the Most Interesting Seeneries That Can Be Found in Zion': Philo Dibble's Museum and Panorama," *Nauvoo Journal* (1997): 25–38.

49. Laura Allred Hurtado and David Grua, "Painting the Mythical and the Heroic: Joseph Preaches to the American Indians," *Juvenile Instructor* (blog), November 19, 2013, https://juvenileinstructor.org.

50. "Moving Pictures: C. C. A. Christensen's Mormon Panorama," June 4-October 3, 2015, curated by Ashlee Whitaker.

51. Laura Allred Hurtado, *Pioneer* 66, no. 1 (2019).

52. R. Devan Jensen, Scott R. Christensen, and Darren Parry, "'Like Fire in the Dry Grass:' Shoshone Conversions and the Christensen Teaching Scroll," *Pioneer* 66, no. 1 (2019): 39–47.

53. Steven C. Harper, *First Vision: Memory and Mormon Origins* (Oxford University Press, 2019), 111.

54. Julie K. Allen, "Mormonism, Gender, and Art in Nineteenth-Century Scandinavia," in *The Routledge Handbook of Mormonism and Gender*, ed. Taylor G. Petrey and Amy Hoyt (Routledge, 2020).

55. Nathan Rees, *Mormon Visual Culture and the American West* (Routledge, 2021).

56. James R. Swensen, "Two Danish Artists—Two Not so Divergent Paths: C. C. A. Christensen, Carl Bloch, and the Evolution of Latter-day Saint Art and Aesthetics," *The Journal of Mormon History* 49, no. 2 (2023): 107–120.

57. Heather Belnap, "Mormon-LDS Art Tradition," in *Variations in Christian Art: Mennonite, Mormon, Quaker, and Swedenborgian*, ed. Diane Apostolos-Cappadona (Bloomsbury Publishing, 2024).

58. Amanda Beardsley and Mason Kamana Allred, eds., *Latter-day Saint Art: A Critical Reader* (Oxford University Press, 2024).

Index

Page references in *italics* denote images.

JENNIFER CHAMPOUX is the director of the Book of Mormon Art Catalog. She is coauthor of *Picturing Christ: Understanding Depictions of Jesus in History and Art* and coeditor of *Approaching the Tree: Interpreting 1 Nephi 8.*

The University of Illinois Press
is a founding member of the
Association of University Presses.

Composed in 10.75/14 Adobe Minion Pro
with DIN display
by Kirsten Dennison
at the University of Illinois Press
Manufactured by Sheridan Books, Inc.

University of Illinois Press
1325 South Oak Street
Champaign, IL 61820-6903
www.press.uillinois.edu